THE COURTS OF HEAVEN FOR BEGINNERS

CHALLENGING FEARS THAT HINDER

LISA NOEL BABBAGE, PHD.

TRILOGY

Trilogy Christian Publishers

A Wholly Owned Subsidiary of Trinity Broadcasting Network

2442 Michelle Drive

Tustin, CA 92780

DEDICATION

To my grandson, Ryder, who is the
manifestation of multiplication, our legacy,
a mother's heart, the promise, and all my joy.

ACKNOWLEDGMENTS

Special thanks to Dr. Camilla Moore for her unending encouragement and friendship as a spiritual sister in Christ. You have dragged me kicking and screaming to an expected end.

To Lydia White, a mission-focused Proverbs 31 wife whose friendship I cherish.

And to my mother, LaNell, who has been a constant cheerleader of all things "underdog," a champion of the cause, and the one who introduced me to my Lord and Savior, Jesus Christ.

TABLE OF CONTENTS

ABOUT THIS BOOK

There is no substitute for a relationship with Jesus Christ as Lord and Savior over your life to see the power of God's kingdom here on earth. Therefore, every person reading this book must understand that the terminology and descriptions herein are based on kingdom principles, which truly only apply to kingdom citizens. That being said, rain falls on all people, whether a saved citizen of heaven or a soul unaware of those things of God. If you consider yourself in the latter group, a person who has not committed themselves to a surrendered life in Christ, it is important that you participate in salvation through a simple prayer of repentance and submission, which triggers the blood of Jesus to stand in the place of penalty for your sin, so that you may share in the heavenly benefit of those who call themselves believers.

Denominations of faith and your knowledge of God's Word have informed your walk in Christ. There will likely be, therefore, differences in denominational teachings or dogma, which may act as distractions to a personal understanding of the ideas outlined in this book. In an effort to overcome any distractions, complications, or interferences that may naturally occur, please understand that I am in no way trying to mess with your theology. The most frustrating thing for the believer is to hear about miracles and even believe in them, never to actually experience a miracle for themselves. Unmet needs in the body of Christ are at an all-time high. How many of us know "good Christians" who "received their healings" by promotion to heaven rather than while here on earth? How much more do we see the poor and hungry in our own communities, the brokenhearted, even in church, and the various crimes and penalties permeating our lives and the lives of those we love? Every single person can likely name a dozen or so situations (think about child abuse, sex trafficking, drug abuse, murder, neglect, corruption, racism, and so on) in which we wish God would act. In other words, we need

1

the miraculous right now. This book is designed to help believers expedite the "time" between a problem and its heavenly solution. It is not a magic formula but rather an insight into a path available to those who are in Christ.

If we overcome by the blood of the Lamb and the word of our testimony, then understand that this book is part of my personal study and testimony. Understand that it is crucial for every hearer of the word of testimony to take advantage of your knowledge that God is no respecter of persons (Romans 2:11–16; Acts 10:34). What is available to one child of God is available to all of God's children regardless of gender, age, ethnicity, denomination, or financial holdings. It is also vitally crucial that we acknowledge the patterns in the Word of God, which are meant for us as mature believers. Things like baptism, tithing, praise, forgiveness, fasting, praying in a spiritual language (tongues), and Communion are all beneficial tools that God gave His church. But if one of these things offends what you understand of faith, know that I do not believe any of those worthy practices are prerequisites to using the ideas in this book to command the miraculous. While I recommend each and every spiritual practice previously listed, such as fasting, tithing, and Communion, if those things are not part of your current spiritual discipline, fear not. I pray our Lord Jesus Christ meets you where you are, opens the eyes of your understanding, awakens your spiritual imagination, and makes the Word alive to you for the application of all those things Christ died to secure for us.

I decided many years ago, after hearing a word of knowledge (a spiritual word or principle that quickened in my spirit when I heard it) from Joyce Meyer, that I wanted every blessing God provides. She said that she decided that if God took the time to record a promise in the Word of God, then it was for her. In other words, if there was a provision in the Word that she wanted or needed, she claimed it. She realized that her being female, uneducated, or any other state in which she found herself did not prohibit her from receiving all God died for. When I heard this, I decided that if it was good enough for Joyce, it was good enough for me, too. To that end, I began to pray what we might call bold prayers. I took faith steps that others might call risky or even foolish. But I understood that I had nothing to lose by doing these things. The scriptures say that God takes the foolish things of this world to confuse the wise. I was content to be foolish in the sight of man because I understood what I could achieve with my own wisdom and that it, my own wisdom, was insufficient for me to do relatively anything.

After thirteen years of practicing this kind of faith and growing as a believer, I experienced not one but two cancer scares. Previously, I overcame cancer through a combination of medicine and miracles, but the treatment was lengthy, leaving me broken and fearful. Everything within me begged not to go through that again. That is when I put my knowledge of the courts of heaven into practice and got a breakthrough that made my previous miracle pale in comparison. Why isn't a miracle a miracle? Aren't I grateful? Of course. But what I learned changed my faith because I saw the power of God not through tears, fears, and longsuffering; instead, I experienced what the heroes of the Bible experienced: an immediate manifestation of favor and recompense.

Consider the man who sat at the pool of Bethesda for thirty-five years waiting for a miracle only to encounter Jesus and be instantly healed (John 5:4). Imagine how this man's life would have been if he had been healed in year one. It would have been a game-changer for him. Now consider Sarah and Abraham, who waited decades for a child. Imagine the relationship between Israel and other Arab nations if Ishmael was never born because they instead received the child of promise, Isaac, in the early years of their marriage (Genesis 16). What about Joseph? Was there another path to Pharaoh, or was the only path to Joseph's destiny through the prison where he experienced heartache, betrayal, and abandonment (Genesis 37)? Like many of you, I concede that God works all things out for our good. His ways are mysterious. But if you, being evil (as the Bible might describe evilness), know how to give good gifts to your children, how much more you're your Father in heaven give to those who believe (Matthew 7:11). In other words, God is able and willing to work with us to solve our problems. In Matthew 9:29 (HCSB), Jesus gave an example I encourage you to take hold of, "Be it unto you according to your faith."

By faith, I intended to receive a healing from cancer quickly. I did not want to spend money on MRIs and doctor's visits for months as I had before. I wanted God to heal me—but I added my desire for a sweatless victory to my prayers and petitions in the mercy courtroom of heaven. There, God spoke to my spirit and said, "Traditional medicine is not the children's bread." I understood this to mean, "Be it unto me according to my faith." Recognize, as you delve into what may be completely new to you, that God does heal through medicine, doctors, technology, prophets, priests, and the like. Even earthly death is a type and shadow of healing because being absent from the body is to be present with the Lord. But imagine how different things could be if we, as mature believers, could circumvent delay and go straight to victory in Jesus.

It is well documented that "those who receive a prophet as a prophet will receive the prophet's reward" (Matthew 10:41, NIV). That can manifest as a faith healer laying hands on someone, and they receive a miracle deliverance. It may also mean a point of contact, such as oil, a cloth, or other vestibule (such as in the Old Testament Tabernacle) that can facilitate a miracle. But imagine, if you will, how this world would change if every mature believer commanded the miraculous as Jesus did. What else could He have meant when He said we would do greater works than these (John 14:12)? God is not waiting on technology, I'm convinced, even though these modern tools are beneficial for the body of Christ. I believe He is waiting on His church to finish building the ark, theoretically speaking, and grow up enough to use every spiritual tool available to us for the edification of the saints, the salvation of the lost, and the cleansing of the bride of Christ. Jesus said that if He be lifted up, He would draw all men to Him (John 12:32). How can we lift Him up when most of us are broke, busted, disgusted, sick, diseased, and bitter? We cannot. That is why I have written this book so that each of us can take dominion over the principalities and powers that so easily beset us.

Many of you may be curious about the courts of heaven as if such an entity cannot be real. As with any supplemental text, let the relationship you have with the Father drive your thoughts and actions. His Word states in Philippians 2:5–11,

> Let this mind be in you which is also in Christ. Who, being in the form of God, thought it not robbery to be equal with God: But made himself of no reputation, and took upon him the form of a servant, and was made in the likeness of men; and being found in fashion as a man, he humbled himself, and became obedient unto death, even the death of the cross. Wherefore God also hath highly exalted him and given him a name which is above every name: That at the name of Jesus every knee should bow, of things in heaven, and things in earth, and things under the earth; and that every tongue should confess that Jesus Christ is Lord, to the glory of God the Father.
>
> Philippians 2:5–11 (KJV)

In this light, we appear before the seat of judgment (2 Corinthians 5:1–10), the heavenly bema, to account for those things, whether good or bad, which we are responsible for. In the same way, we have a manifestation of the heavenly judgment here on earth of that which is recorded in the heavenly courtroom. Since God is the Creator of all things and repetitively references legal terminology in His Word, this author yields to the idea that not only are the courts of heaven very real, but they are also open to us who believe. According to John 3:18,

Whoever believes, and has decided to trust in Him [Jesus, as personal Savior and Lord] is not judges, or rather condemned; but the one who does not believe, *and in effect has rejected Jesus as Lord and Savior,* is already judged because he had not believed... as Jesus is the One who alone can save.

John 3:18 (AMP)

This is not a book about deliverance but rather a guide into a legal journey that brings with it a type of recompense of reward that is akin to spiritual emancipation from not only the fears that hinder us in our walk with God but also from the generational assault our enemy wages daily. It is intended for those who have done all they know to do and are now standing on a promise or biblical principle (and are growing weary). It is not for the faint of heart because who among us of a wavering mind can hope to achieve any (good) thing? As with all legal proceedings, there is a specific court to which we may present our grievances. From the position of the plaintiff or defendant, we may also see remuneration for our suffering. And as with any legal proceeding, an admission of guilt is entered for the record, as is evidence, witnesses, pleas, and decrees.

In conclusion, we expect a just verdict, a self-executing order, from the Just Judge, who is our righteousness and our reward. Oftentimes, we question new expressions of biblical disciplines that are outside of our current practices. Understand that this book is written with the understanding that in God's mercy, He hears our prayers and petitions, yet according to His Word, which is His bond, there are times when we do not receive because we pray amiss (James 4:3). Every promise in the Word of God is "yes and amen" yet to every season there is a time under heaven (2 Corinthians 1:20; Ecclesiastes 3). God has declared that blessings overtake us because nothing is impossible with God, yet there are still seeds, time, and harvest (Deuteronomy 28:2; Luke 1:37;

Genesis 8:22), which may appear as a delay in the things of God. First Corinthians 12:31 speaks of the more excellent way of the kingdom of heaven, better than the best gifts, better by far, and highest of them all: love. Love for the Father and having the Father's heart for people, I believe, grants us access to the legal ministry of the kingdom of God, which works in conjunction with our faith to expedite those things the Holy Spirit reveals to us in the Communion of the saints for the fulfilling of God's kingdom here on earth. In other words, this is not a new way to pray. It is with this understanding that I encourage you to petition the courts of heaven as you are urged to do so by God's Holy Spirit. As you do, pray in your heavenly language as well as in your earthly language because you know God works all things out for your good in His system of justice.

Let me credit Robert Henderson, who has done much research in the area of the courts of heaven, for the following truths. You do not need a special seer anointing to operate in the courts of heaven. It is within God's desire that the wrongful accusations and judgments against us be annulled through the blood of Jesus. It is the Holy Spirit who acts as our legal counsel in the courts, enduing us with groanings that speak to God's purpose for us. We can work by faith toward the plans God has for us in this world. Finally, it is the developed relationship with our Lord Jesus Christ that results in the perpetual audience with the Just Judge, our king, and our God so that in His righteousness, we might receive our reward through Him that works in us.

ONE

HOME-COURT ADVANTAGE

Psychologically speaking, home-court advantage occurs when travel, logistics, climate, and time zones change, and other idiosyncrasies impact an athlete's ability to perform or participate in their sport to their fullest potential. The physiological advantage of playing near home in familiar settings can be the difference between success and failure for the player and the team. It is the same reason why people tend to stick with what works, with what's familiar. When we find a restaurant that prepares our favorite dish the way we like it, or when we find great service, we tend to revisit that establishment again and again. In the same way, we have an advantage when we seek out and utilize the home-court benefit in Christ.

There is an old proverb from Jesus's Sermon on the Mount that states, "For He [the Father] makes His sun to rise on the evil and on the good and sends rain on the just and on the unjust. For this cause, Jesus said, love your enemies, bless those that curse you, and pray for them that despitefully persecute you" (Matthew 5:44–45, ESV). For as most Christians understand, we war not against flesh and blood but against principalities in high places.

It has been said time and time again that the battle of good versus evil, which is evident in the stories of the Bible as well as in the life of every believer, is a type of war. Furthermore, we have heard that Jesus's blood has won the war for us. Yet battles, like the valleys in life, are ours to engage in daily. In fact, there are so many references in scripture to the battles we as believers engage in that one cannot help but draw a military comparison. To that conclusion, Ephesians 6:13–18 describes the spiritual battle armor believers must wear in order to endure the warfare we experience against principalities in high places. While there is a time for everything in its season, both war and peace have their courses in heaven and on earth.

Why, then, is home-court advantage important when the war is already won and most believe the battle isn't even theirs?

While there is truth in the finished victories in Christ, there can be no doubt that there are daily battles every person encounters because of the relentlessness of our adversary and accuser. The scripture says in Job 2,

> The LORD said to Satan, "Have you considered *and* reflected on My servant Job? For there is none like him on the earth, a blameless and upright man, one who fears God [with reverence] and abstains from *and* turns away from evil [because he honors God]. And still he maintains *and* holds tightly to his integrity, although you incited Me against him to destroy him without cause."
>
> Job 2:3 (AMP)

If the blameless and upright man is a God-inspired target of our adversary, how then can we expect to be exempt from daily battles? We cannot. In fact, we should consider it a badge of honor when we endure a battle and come out on the other side of the field with our faith intact.

In 1865, Sabine Baring-Gould, an Anglican priest, wrote one of many hymns during his travels throughout Europe and while teaching in his native England. "Onward Christian Soldiers," a song inspired by the children he saw walking in uniform to school daily, is built on 2 Timothy 2:3 (KJV), "Thou therefore endure hardness, as a good soldier of Jesus Christ." This reference is yet another correlation to the military nature of our interactions with the enemy of our faith. The song was adopted by The Salvation Army as their preferred processional hymn and was chosen by Winston Churchill in a church service concluding the Atlantic Charter after World War II. He said,

We sang "Onward, Christian Soldiers" indeed, and I felt that this was no vain presumption, but that we had the right to feel that we were serving a cause for the sake of which a trumpet has sounded from on high. When I looked upon that densely packed congregation of fighting men of the same language, of the same faith, of the same fundamental laws, of the same ideals ... it swept across me that here was the only hope, but also the sure hope, of saving the world from measureless degradation.

"A cause for the sake of the trumpet" is the high calling of the gospel, which is good news. In other words, it is a worthy cause we as believers are bound to endure so that when we meet our great reward in heaven, we can hear those long-cherished words, "Well done." Yet in these battles, as in life, there will be trouble. That is why a well-equipped soldier will utilize home-court advantage in order to defeat the adversary on every side.

Let me outline the practical application of this spiritual principle. Much of what we encounter as believers is based on our choices. However, when providence, meaning God's direction over the universe and the affairs of mankind, collides with free will, supernatural things happen. We often call these occurrences miraculous, but science might add to that definition. A miracle is defined by Webster as an effect or extraordinary event in the physical that surpasses all known human or natural power and is therefore described as supernatural. But when we consider the laws of science and mathematics that identify verifiable and replicated outcomes as law, a prescribed outcome, not chance, we can glean a deeper understanding of the miraculous. For example, two plus two will always equal four, no matter what. This is not a coincidence; it is a mathematical law.

In the same way, spiritually and practically speaking, miracles should not be counted as mere possibilities. Miracles are how God prefers to interact with us. When we battle against our enemy, God's intention is that we war in tandem with Him. It was for this cause that Christ bled and rose from the pit. It was to empower us or give us home-court advantage over our opponent.

If two plus two will always equal four, if gravity always causes an object to fall to the ground, then when free will aligns with God's providence, a miracle will *always* occur. Why, then, do we seem to see fewer miracles in modern times than in times past when Jesus clearly said we would do more? Good question. One you've probably asked yourself. First and foremost, there are likely many unrecorded miracles happening every day in the present time. But let's deal with the battle at hand. Whatever the need be, whatever you are facing today, that's the miracle in which you are expecting a breakthrough. Everything else is just icing on an already-baked cake.

Perhaps, like me, you have done all you know to do and are standing on the Word of God for a miraculous manifestation in your situation. Well done, Christian soldier. Now, let's understand home-court advantage as a means to accessing the courts of heaven for greater breakthroughs. Let's face it. We can war and stand until the cows come home. But when we do not use the full resources Christ's death and resurrection gave us access to, then we are leaving blessings on the table. Why else, let me propose, are we as believers in the situations in which we find ourselves globally? As of this writing, the church has been a faithful sojourner divided against itself through denominationalism and largely operating in ignorance of the power of the five-fold ministry of God.

That does not mean that we, as faithful believers in Christ, have not operated genuinely with one another. It does suggest, however, that we are missing a big part of what it means to bring the kingdom of heaven here to earth. Perhaps the idea of bringing heaven here is a foreign concept to you. Consider Jesus's words in the model prayer given in Matthew 6. "Thy will be done on earth as it is in heaven" (Matthew 6:10, KJV). Without a doubt, earth is a far cry from heaven. Not only are we dealing with potholes while a great cloud of witnesses walks on streets of gold, but the body of Christ is not united, and we see the effects of it around the world. It is my contention that in order for the bridegroom to receive His spotless church, we must unite in the understanding of our power and role on earth. In other words, we must operate in the home-court advantage Christ died for us to have when he gave us the "keys of the kingdom of heaven, and [so ordered that] whatever you bind on earth shall be bound in heaven, and whatever you loose on earth shall be loosed in heaven" (Matthew 16:19, NASB). This is the open reward of the victory that overcomes the world, even our faith.

How can we order something without the legal authority to do so? We cannot. Yet even with legal authority and the right purpose, these proceedings are only legitimate in the hearing of those who can carry out the orders. That is why home-court advantage is so powerful. We have the opportunity of calling a great cloud of witnesses to testify on our behalf. They can do more than just cheer us on from the rafters because home-court advantage is more than just a stadium of loyal fans. It is the logistical, chronological, material, geographical, and metaphysical advantage of our position as followers of Jesus. Children of the Most High God. Sons and daughters.

It almost sounds too good to be true, doesn't it? Okay, let the Word of God confirm these words in your heart. Therefore, as newly ranked generals in the faith, you can lead Christian soldiers into the victory to which they have been given in Christ here on earth in this present time.

Perhaps you do not consider yourself "general" material. Welcome to the club. Consider this: every general was once a private. Abraham, Moses, Peter, John, and all of the disciples we revere as generals of faith were common men who took an uncommon God at His word. Almost overnight, every biblical hero and heroine was promoted in rank when they accepted and understood the position to which they were called. You, too, can embark on this journey of promotion and expect to see the miraculous occur routinely, just as routinely as knowing two and two will equal four.

Not convinced? Neither was I, initially. When I heard the call of the Lord in my spirit, I assumed it was a pity offering. I debated, for months, perhaps years, with the Holy Spirit about what I understood about myself and others. As a member of the production team at my church, I was blessed to hear and record ministers from around the world who spoke at our various conferences. However, hearing great teaching was not enough to convince me that I was hearing God clearly.

When Priscilla Shirer stood in our church's pulpit, I reminded God that He already had a very dynamic Black female on His team. I told God, in case He forgot, that she came with the pedigree of a well-adored servant-leader father. Surely, she was sufficient to reach every Black woman out there. Her father could cover the men, I mused. To these ramblings, God was immovable in His messaging to me.

When Christine Caine spoke at a certain conference, I reminded God that He already had an Australian female minister who had real-world training from a planet-shaking church. I told Him that Christine had a lot of energy and passion let in her—something I felt was lacking in myself. Again, God did not relent. When Sarah Jakes spoke, I reminded God He already had a woman whose early decisions resonated with the brokenness of urban America. When Gloria Copeland taught, I reminded Him that there was already a Southern teacher on the team. When Lisa Bevere lectured, I reminded Him He already had a "Lisa." In other words, I looked for every excuse not to believe God needed me to spread His Word. Minister after minister, I pointed God's attention to. Someone else was always more equipped than me in my own eyes. Yet, I kept sensing the urge in my spirit to do more to get the good news of the gospel to the world. "Why, God," I asked, "are You calling me?"

Priscilla Shirer was preaching in Gainesville, Georgia, when I asked that last question. I had spent the entire conference watching her maneuver flawlessly across the stage with her wireless microphone. Her trademark curls were in place, again flawlessly, as was her makeup. As she spoke about her husband Jerry and their boys, telling stories and relating them to scripture, executing perfectly timed hand gestures, the gravitas rose in the room. That's when God spoke to my heart, and I knew in that moment that everyone *was* created for a purpose. We were created to be light in the darkness, to be witnesses for God. Frankly, if one witness could reach everyone, you and I would not be here. In fact, no one would. Because the first disciples, John and Andrew, could've taken care of the mission. Every minister since them has taught the same message. Is there still a need for more when so many great men and women have technology at their disposal to preach the gospel to the entire world? The answer most definitely is a resounding yes because until we see "on earth as it is in heaven," we're not done. No matter who your audience is, hundreds, thousands, or just the handful in your own home, there is a need for your witness. Ultimately, your witness is not just about the good news but is also about equipping the saints in their battles.

This year, I found myself watching a YouTube video of Priscilla Shier. It simply popped up in my feed. She started off with a disclaimer as she addressed a room full of women in ministry, which intrigued me. Five minutes into this talk she said the words I never thought I would hear from her: "I struggle." Years before, when I watched her flawlessly engage a two-thousand-person audience, I would've never guessed she struggled at anything. Yet here she was, being open, honest, and transparent about how grace moved in her public life. I was encouraged.

Parents fight to provide a home for their children. They advocate for their education and rights in society. A greater purpose awaits in fighting spiritual battles for our young ones. Add to this those young in faith and those bound to us by covenant, contract, and grace who rely on spiritual victories to stand, therefore. This is a mantle to which we who are mature in faith, that is, steadfast in our beliefs, have been called and must be willing to pursue. In this mission field, we have to rest in the knowledge that God's grace will meet us where we are and can take us where God wants us to go. The only question that remains is how long it will take us to get there.

I will never forget the first time I saw my family crest, which was designed by my grandfather, an Anglican priest. He included the words *I press on* from Philippians 3:14 as part of the epitaph he spoke over his lineage. The Bible clearly expresses that if Jesus were to tarry or delay His return, even the elect would fall away, their ability to press on cut short due to the daily battles of faith we are required to engage in. "Elect" in this context means those who have been determined beforehand or ordained for salvation. Like any sheep in a herd, there are mature and immature, weak and strong among the flock. Each has been determined beforehand, from the womb, to be sheep. Yet, inevitably, some will fall to the slaughter.

As we, globally, serve as members of a divided flock, it is incumbent upon us to gather the young in spirit and war on their behalf. In this great challenge, we are remiss not to utilize home-court advantage in these battles. For this to become real to me, I had to shift my perspective when it came to my worth and the perceived worth of platform ministers. Sometimes, we think that God favors one over another. We assume He can use some more than others because of some talent or gifting. The truth is that God has made room for each of us in His kingdom. In fact, He has a plan for each one of us, a mission specifically designed for the person we are in Him. There is no spiritual rank we cannot achieve if we only put everything in submission to God's will. This I firmly believe. Otherwise, why would he have written in His Word that "[in Christ] there is neither Jew nor Greek, there is neither bond nor free, there is neither male nor female: for you are all one in Christ Jesus. And if you are Christ's, then are you

Abraham's seed, and heirs according to the promise" (Galatians 3:28-29, HCSB). To that end, understand that the benefits of Christ's death and resurrection are also without repentance and are available to all who call Him Lord and Savior.

LOGISTICAL HOME-COURT ADVANTAGE

In a word, logistics is procurement. The military science definition also deals with the maintenance and transportation of personnel, facilities, and materials. "To procure" is a transitive verb that is primarily a military one and involves permissions and transferring ownership or possession from a higher governing body to a lower one. We might make a spiritual comparison to the help and helpers given us as believers in the examples found in scripture that originate in the Lord's Prayer: on earth as it is in heaven. That is a picture of the higher governing body in heaven as it relates to the lower governing body on earth.

First, we must make clear the caretakers of the logistical home-court advantage. The first chapter of Genesis outlines God's initial plan for mankind. Verses 27–28 give two important truths we must apply to our knowledge of warfare and authority.

> So, God created mankind in his own image, in the image of God he created them; male and female he created them.
>
> God blessed them and said to them, "Be fruitful and increase in number; fill the earth and subdue it. Rule over the fish in the sea and the birds in the sky and over every living creature that moves on the ground."
>
> Genesis 1:27–28 (NIV)

The passage begins by establishing the authority through whom you and I find our position or allegiance. Humanity was created in two forms, male and female, in one image, God's. That fact is restated in the verse for emphasis and confirmation. In other words, there should be no question about identity because it was established from the very beginning by the Creator, or initiator, of humanity itself. To the pair to whom He bestowed the blessing of authority, He gives these four commands: increase, fill, subdue, and rule. These are all government or military commands, as well as mathematical ones. Before going too deep into home-court advantage, let's learn about two norms in God's kingdom that were present when humanity reigned earth in totality.

THE POWER OF AGREEMENT

Adam and Eve, the first of humanity, had a special relationship with God, one that we, as descendants, have birthright access to: the power of agreement. We must be perfectly clear that God wants us to be of one mind in Him, even as Jesus and the Father are of one mind. This is, perhaps, where the power of agreement begins. The Old Testament books of Deuteronomy, Leviticus, and Joshua all share the verse that talks about the power of agreement. One will put a thousand to flight, but two can put infinitely more...a thousand, ten thousand. God's Word states we will do exceedingly more than Jesus did. How is this possible unless we agree with the plans of the Lord? The power of agreement is crucial not only to home-court advantage but to accessing the courts of heaven in any capacity. We are foolish if we expect to move God's hand against His will. Knowing this, we should begin to see the reason why God loves community so much.

In Moses's leadership, we see God take a special interest in making sure the community of Israel was in one accord. When they weren't, God delayed their purpose. James 1:8 (KJV) says, "A double minded man [-kind] is unstable in all his ways." In other words, if a group is not in agreement, their plans falter and can fail. Instability is their portion. This can be evident in business, family, community, or intimate relationships. God wouldn't have said to love your neighbor as you love yourself if He hadn't intended for us to work together (Mark 12:31). You might even go further to hypothesize that it is not God but God's ruling that causes the double-minded to delay. After all, like gravity and multiplication tables, there are expected outcomes to the laws and ordinances God established during creation.

Let's look at another example of agreement from the Garden of Eden. When Adam and Eve fell to sin, their special relationship, which was in one accord with God, began to deteriorate. Eventually, they fell asleep in death, which was not God's best for them. It took their bodies hundreds of years to get there, but the separation from Christ through sin decreased the power of agreement in their lives. Their one consolation was the ability to agree with one another. After all, they had been made in God's image and still remembered the power they had before sin—God's original intent.

After sin, however, the punishment for sin introduced a different kind of agreement. The third chapter of Genesis details the loss of authority and dominion to sin. Some translations offer a subtitle beginning with verse 8, stating, "God Arraigned Adam and Eve." Before they were expulsed from the garden, their verdict was delivered:

> To the woman He said:
>
> "I will sharply increase your pain in childbirth;
>
> in pain you will bring forth children.
>
> Your desire will be for your husband,
>
> and he will rule over you."
>
> And to Adam He said:
>
> "Because you have listened to the voice of your wife
>
> and have eaten from the tree
>
> of which I commanded you not to eat,
>
> cursed is the ground because of you;

through toil you will eat of it
all the days of your life.

Both thorns and thistles it will yield for you,
and you will eat the plants of the field.

By the sweat of your brow
you will eat your bread,

until you return to the ground—
because out of it were you taken.

For dust you are,
and to dust you shall return."

Genesis 3:16–19 (BSB)

Seems a bit harsh for eating one little piece of fruit. I know I felt that way the first time I read that story as a child. But God's precepts and rules were more than just a test for Adam and Eve. I believe the tree represented the tithe, that which belongs to or is returned to God. Shall a man rob God? Certainly not. Neither shall God's children act in disobedience without consequence. The fact is that God addresses part of Adam and Eve's curse in Malachi 3:8–12 when He offers the windows of heaven in exchange for obedience. God promises to rebuke the devourer and multiply the harvest from the ground for simple obedience. But His statutes and ordinances are not about obedience for obedience's sake alone. Typically, these laws are put in place for our betterment. Whether it is for the poor, the widowed, the sick, or for our own mental and spiritual health, God calls us to agree with Him and those bound to us by covenant, contract, and grace so that it may be well with us. Simple as that. He has a better way to do things. But the power of agreement is only one-half of the specific benefit Christ gave back to us when He redeemed us from the curse issued in the garden.

THE SPIRIT OF AUTHORITY

Here we go back to Adam and Eve; after all, they constitute the first geological measure of the redemptive history narrative. In Genesis, God's covenant with mankind resulted in a shared authority between Adam and his wife as God's ambassadors on earth. They were given the same power to exercise dominion. God even commanded them to rule over all life (Genesis 1:28–30). That is what dominion means: kingdom domain. It's as if God is saying, "Behold, look! This is all yours." As co-ruler, Eve was dependent on Adam's partnership. Adam knew that either of them had the power to rebuke the speaking serpent instead of entertaining his foolishness and trickery. As the saying goes, if you play with fire, you will eventually get burned. Adam and Eve certainly got burned spiritually and put us all at risk for eternal damnation.

Notice how God's sentencing of Eve was much shorter than Adam's after they disobeyed Him. She had been on equal footing with Adam and, as a result of sin, was demoted to second in the hierarchy. "Your desire will be for your husband..." the scripture says, demonstrating the joint leadership that they shared, which ended when he said, "... and he will rule over you" (Genesis 3:16, BSB). Women today continue to vie for the same authority as men in every sector. Yet, in most instances, men still rule over them. This is how the curse manifested itself for her. There was also the matter of childbirth, which, while under attack worldwide today, was the special task God gave Eve. Because of the curse, that task now brings pain and, for some, death. Adam's penalty and loss of authority were far more reaching.

The ground is actually accursed as a part of Adam's lost authority. Mankind was given dominion by our Creator at the time of our first breath. But when Adam gave authority to our enemy through sin, the earth and all things created fell under the curse. Romans 8:22–24 warns that all earth groans as with the pains of childbirth. Another way of saying that is that because of lost authority, even the dust of the earth from which we were formed yearns to return to the garden state to end this present suffering. We return to dust when we leave this earth, but who's to say that even the dust of human bodies did not yearn for redemption before Christ? Yet, through Christ, the power of agreement is reinstituted. When the price for the sin-generating curse was paid, it, the curse, was finished. On the cross, Jesus spoke seven expressions in His final moments. These words concluded with, "Father, into your hands I commit my spirit" (Luke 23:46, NIV). He put our spirits back with the Spirit from which we were born, redeeming the curse and reinstituting the power of agreement along with the dominion initially granted in the garden. Not only do we have the Spirit of authority with Jesus, our intermediary, but we also have the power to agree with God and our fellow man to re-establish dominion here on earth.

When God calls us to increase (be fruitful) and fill (multiply) the earth, He does so from a position of dominion. In the beginning was God, most followers agree, and the earth was without form and void, which is described in Genesis. This scripture is confirmed or supported by Psalm 139, which describes the omnipresence and omniscience of God. It states, "You knit me together in my mother's womb" (Psalm 139:13, NIV). It speaks of God's foreknowledge of each of us. The logistics of our humanity were formed by God's own hand in the darkness of the womb. As cells divide and fill from the placenta, they dominate the space in which the child grows and develops, directing the mother's body to participate in the birthing process until it is complete. How else does the Bible support this idea of logistical home-court advantage beyond these examples? Well, it is clear that God's divine involvement in creation includes birthing, but it may not be obvious how God has created systems through which we can procure the blessings of liberty and freedom under grace.

As believers in Christ's ministry, it is necessary that we operate in the kingdom principles Jesus demonstrated here on earth and in His Word. For example, the miracle of the fish and the loaves was a logistical miracle as well as a creative one. When Jesus blessed the meal, His disciples, being in one accord or agreement, were able to procure provision for the crowd by aligning their faith with divinity. After all, the food multiplied in their hands, not the Savior's (Matthew 14:13–21). Furthermore, when Jesus instructed the attendees to sit in groups of fifties and hundreds, He mirrored a military sectioning common to the Department of Defense armed force's organizational structure. It is important to further investigate the logistical home-court advantage of this miracle that began with a young man's snack.

For all intents and purposes, we have no proof positive of what kind of fish were provided, but we do know the quantities of each kind of food. This is a type of logistical notation because every line item in procurement requires a specific quantity. Even the crowd was given a numerical value. Why else would the disciples record the number of attendees if logistics were not in play? Before the miracle, it really shouldn't have mattered how many were there, whether twelve or twelve thousand. Because in their natural circumstance, they could not feed anyone. But when their faith encountered Jesus's blessing, they entered into a logistical home-court advantage by faith through proximity.

In the breaking of the fish and loaves, they procured a sample of the materials needed to participate in the miracle. By themselves, they had no "seed" or sample of the food needed, which is why they initially asked Jesus to send the crowd away so that they could find food on their own. As a group of church leaders, they were not expecting a miracle, but one of them took a donation from another in proximity, the young man. They transferred ownership of the snack lunch to Jesus, causing the earthly seed to interact with heaven through Christ. The need was surrendered, and ownership was transferred from the boy to the disciples to God. Sounds like a tithe, doesn't it? It also sounds like a community of faith. Truth be known, each of those attendees didn't have to sit around waiting for a crumb from the boy's lunch. Especially for those sitting in the back, there was no guarantee that the loaves and fish would still multiply when the disciples eventually got to them. How many of us would have yielded to hunger pains and simply left the meeting early? If we think about it, it probably happens every Sunday in every church, as members leave early to get ahead of lunchtime crowds at our favorite restaurants.

Even though this was not the only miraculous feeding described in Scripture, it is unique in the nature of how the miracle was carried out. When Jesus fed the 4,000 followers described in Matthew 15:32–39 and Mark 8:1–9, it was He who felt compassion for the hungry attendees. In the previous, more famous miracle, it was the disciples who, after hearing the people's groans, sought Jesus for a solution to the problem. In other words, this logistical miracle occurred when one member of the body sought to meet the needs of another. Perhaps the impact of this work was so great that the gospel writers all recognized the order in which God operates for the first time. Besides the resurrection, this miracle is the only one recorded by all four authors.

Furthermore, the act is given much more emphasis, considering that it is one of only ten events in Jesus's ministry substantiated in all four gospels. Aside from the start of Jesus's ministry and His death, this event stands alone as being singled out. Logistically speaking, it is in a class by itself. It documents the advantage of proximity to Christ to meet the needs brought before Him with a seed in hand. That is the essence of logistics. Transferring ownership of their borrowed lack (think about your personal circumstance as you ponder the idea of borrowed lack), along with a petition regarding an unmet need, moved Christ enough to procure manifestation for the multitude in the hands of the disciples. Again, this is the essential function of logistics.

Cell division was mentioned earlier to show how God can create matter from matter. From the very beginning, He took His spoken Word and His (creatively empowered) breath to create the heavens and the earth. He took the dust off the ground and made man. He fashioned woman from the rib of man. In each example, He took matter to recreate matter. Science has proven that a zygote, a female egg, and spermatozoa combine to create a new human. The moon, sun, seas, seasons, and all creation in their courses are evidence that Creator God uses existing matter to create more or new matter. Even the stars, the Hubble Telescope revealed, are born from stellar nurseries after their own kind. This pattern of procurement, which is repeated throughout recorded and pre-recorded history, demonstrates the logistical nature of God as well as our ability to operate within logistical patterns to have a home-court advantage eligible to produce multitude-sized miracles in our hands. Yes, God is the Creator. However, logistical miracles access storehouses in heaven, which transfer ownership from God to His image-bearers. In other words, once God creates something, He need not create it again, only procure it from His stockpiles and transfer ownership once the spiritual requisition of need has been heard.

Can you imagine what it means to have the windows of heaven (Malachi 3:10) open on your behalf? It is this concept of storehouses, or saving, that is crucial to the concept of logistical home-court advantage. Jeremiah 51:16 (AMP) records that "He makes lightnings for the rain. And brings out the wind from His storehouses." These storehouses are further confirmed by Psalm 139, which reminds us that we were foreknown by Him who made us. This is an attribution of the fact that there is intentional planning in heaven for creative purposes. The parallel of the patterns and systems in the earth mirror that which was created by heaven, modeled in the earthly kingdom. If we who cannot answer our own prayers have enough sense to plan for the future, why do we struggle to imagine that heaven has planned for our future? The building block of all things created, DNA, is a blueprint by which the master carpenter may build, fashion, or replicate that which has already been created. Why else, one might ask, would He go ahead of us and make our crooked ways straight, according to Jeremiah 29? All of these representations, and many more, are logistical in nature. We, as children of the Most High, have access to the logistical system of heaven, which provides us with an advantage over our enemy in this earthly realm; it is but one of the ways in which we can transcend our earthly shackles and engage as citizens of heaven have a blood-bought right to.

CHRONOLOGICAL HOME-COURT ADVANTAGE

It has already been referenced that nature evolves in cyclical patterns in heaven and earth according to Genesis 8:22. These cycles speak of the order that God has established. We can characterize that order by the predictability of things we see. For example, the sun rises in the east and sets in the west, moving in a horizontal line across our periphery. This is something neither weather forecasters nor meteorologists have to wonder about. No matter where you are in the world or what language you speak, the surety of the sun is not something you doubt.

There are multi-step cycles, such as the life cycle of a butterfly, which has a terminal end, and the water cycle, which repeats itself without end, rewatering the earth as it did thousands of years ago. There is a time and place for these cycles to occur, but there are also cycles that can be initiated by humanity. For example, there are at least twenty verses that reference "reaping" in the Word of God. Whether we focus on the seed, which can be words or deeds that initiate a growth cycle, the chronology of the cycle itself (time), or the harvest, which is that benefit we seek (or conversely, the curse we have sewn into), there is a role both heaven and earth play in the reaping; and the order of reaping is something God initiates. He created man after and in His likeness. Therefore, every seed produces after its own kind. This is a predictable cycle that not only shatters the idea of evolution as a replacement for creation but also solidifies the identity to which you and I are born. We are image-bearers of God and called gods in our own right through the inheritance we receive as kingdom citizens united under the banner of Christ's shed blood.

In order to understand what is meant by chronological home-court advantage, it is important to know first and foremost that God is the one who gives seed to the sower (2 Corinthians 9:10); furthermore, He increases our seed to enlarge the harvest for our righteousness. What that means is that the seed is for more than just our personal benefit; it is designed to be enlarged for righteousness' sake. Righteousness is characterized by uprightness, morally correct or justifiable. Its origins lay not only in truth but wisdom. The righteous, as a collective, are described as being conscientious, ethical, blameless, matchless, pure, and virtuous. These adjectives, of course, could not be assigned to us without being filtered through the blood of Jesus; it is His righteousness that makes us righteous, as a state of being in Him.

So, when we consider that seed, which is the springboard for reaping, takes place in time for the sake of the collective righteous ones, we can begin to appreciate the communal nature of the life we are supposed to command here on earth. That, my friends, is especially where a chronological home-court advantage can be a game changer. Let's consider a practical example before diving deeper into the spiritual benefits Christ died for us to have.

When a sports team flips a coin to determine who will receive the ball, it is a home-court advantage of timing when that coin falls in their favor. Likewise, in a game of baseball, the home team always bats second, giving them the benefit of batting last in the eighth inning. Being last to bat in baseball is a chronological home-court advantage, just like a coin flip can determine receivership or service. These are all issues of timing. Timing is more than sports—timing plays a role in nature, the arts, medicine, government, education, religion, and family. Some say, "Timing is everything." While that may or may not be true, one thing we can likely all agree on is that timing is important. For example, paying your student loan after the deadline assigns a monetary penalty to your account and credit because you paid late: an issue of timing. When we petition the courts after the statute of limitations has expired, our claim, no matter how valid, is not even considered because time has run out. Early harvesting of fruit can cause the pit to become bitter in storage. Each of these negative examples is impacted by time. However, timing can also be a good thing. For example, the principal dancer in a ballet company (prima or primo ballerina) appears first in a group, but not only first: he or she remains on stage the longest. The first invention, or occurrence, is forever credited with the discovery and achievement. In other words, chronology is related not only to rank but to rating as well.

First Corinthians 15:23 reports that Christ is the first fruit of the resurrection, and we, in turn, as believers, are numbered subsequent to Him. Because He was the first and only, His name remains above all names. Yet, we are counted or accredited with Him by association. Practically speaking, that means that believers who invoke Christ's blood as a part of our salvation package receive the benefit of being first. This is the home-court advantage that may manifest in the areas of our finances, relationships, health, wisdom, purpose, and passion. Some time ago, I sensed the Holy Spirit telling me to amend a common prayer I prayed to acknowledge the grace given through my Communion with the First Fruit. For years, I prayed for those bound to me by covenant, contract, or blood as a catch-all way of covering my family, friends, co-workers, and business associates so that it may be well with me. My personal and professional life was full of strife, and I desperately wanted it to come to a desired conclusion. The spiritual weight weighed heavily on me prior to committing to this simple statement in prayer. However, years into this practice, the Holy Spirit challenged me to add those bound to be "by grace" to that daily petition as a game changer to purpose. It opened my eyes to the bigger mission that God has called me to in time. After adding the grace community to my daily prayer, I have begun to see the importance of time in "seed time and harvest" because it is the grace of our Lord Jesus Christ that can accelerate time for our favor. Just as we have confidence that salvation is a free gift, we must also understand that the reason that Jesus is the same yesterday, today, and forever is that He is not subject to time. He changes not because time will never change Him. We are the ones who, if time delayed, would be susceptible to growing weary in well doing (Galatians 6:9). We risk bending again to a yoke of slavery (Galatians 5:1) in time. We are charged with returning again to our first love (Revelation 2:4; Matthew 24:12) because we have waxed cold in our spiritual fervor over time. Example after example is given in Scripture that acknowledges the fickleness of our flesh in time, that in weakness, we must be restored to the Spirit (Matthew 26:41).

We must acknowledge the seasons and times appointed to us. The significance thereof is not merely acknowledged so we, like the wise virgins, can be prepared for the things to come but so we can command or mandate the advantage that Christ died for us to have.

In Scripture, chronology not only means time but also folds, seasons, hours, occasions, generations, ages, courses, and cycles. By definition, a fold is a type of multiplication that is less likely to perform cyclically. However, cycle, course, and season are all cyclical time frames. A generation may be a specific period of time or times depending on the context, while the hour and occasion are terminal events with everlasting impact. Each of these measures of time gives believers an advantage in this age in which we live. Previous generations grew their own food and tended their own flocks. They hunted and gathered grain. Their lives were consumed with survival. In this dispensation of time, we have the benefit of invention and technology that gives both men and women the option of utilizing modern conveniences that free up time for us. However, we are remiss to relegate time as being spent or saved without understanding the times in which we live: a time that demands we utilize chronology as a tool to bring about the swift return of our Lord and Savior. This is established in the kingdom of our God and by example of His power given to us as ambassadors of His kingdom.

GEOGRAPHICAL HOME-COURT ADVANTAGE

The High Priestly Prayer found in John outlines Jesus's desire and petition for us. The entire chapter is a red-letter prayer to heaven on our behalf. It is important to note one of the key principles within this prayer found in Chapter 17:14–16.

> I have given to them Your word [the message You gave Me] [Christ states to the Father regarding us], and the world has hated them because they are not of the world *and* do not belong to the world, just as I am not of the world *and* do not belong to it. I do not ask You to take them out of the world, but that You keep them *and* protect them from the evil one. They are not of the world, just as I am not of the world.
>
> John 17:14–16 (AMP, author's clarification)

Our geography, Jesus says, is not of this world, although we are clearly in this world. While that reference may be well known to you, just as the other twenty references regarding the duality in which we exist, it is unlikely you have considered the geographical advantages of this dual citizenship privilege you enjoy.

My father is an Australian citizen, and although he has maintained his permanent residency status in the United States, he is still an Australian. He no longer has a foreign accent. He dresses like an American and retired from an American company. He married an American woman and has adopted the culture in which he lives. Despite all of his appearances and habits, he is a foreigner—his rights and privileges ultimately lie within the jurisdiction of his birth country. For instance, he must register with the US Immigration and Naturalization Service every ten years or so. He cannot vote and has no legal representation in the American government because he is not a citizen. His residency status is contingent upon him obeying the laws in the country in which he resides. His (American) privilege is limited based on his residency status, which is less than the advantages a full citizen would have. However, as his child, I enjoy not only the full privilege of the nation of my birth but the nation of his birth as well. I have a legal right to dual citizenship and irrevocable citizenship from both nations. Jesus's death and resurrection grant us the same access to dual citizenship as residents of the earth who have been reborn from heaven. This occurs when we accept Jesus as Lord and Savior. The forms, costs, and petitions were made in the thirty-nine stripes He bore on His back. The chastisement of our peace being laid upon Him in the form of crucifixion, which is a capital punishment or judicial homicide. Capital punishments are state-sanctioned, meaning that a governing body authorizes the condemnation to death. In the case of believers, it is Jesus who secured our citizenship through the mutual consent of heaven (God's kingdom) and Himself (God in flesh), as well as the government under which He lived on earth.

To explore the geographical home-court advantage of being a citizen of heaven, begin by embracing the notion that we (set-apart ones) cannot flee from the presence of the Lord because His Spirit seeks out the things of the Lord in order to fulfill His promises. God is both omnipresent and omniscient (Psalm 139). David recorded that God is intimately acquainted with all our ways. This is crucial as it illustrates not only the sovereignty of God but our relationship with Him. A way of looking at that in the natural is to understand the rights and privileges due to Prince Harry and Prince William by birth. The monarchs of England have had a lasting impression over nearly every continent. Yet, the youngest royals are known for a reason other than their ability to lead. They are Diana's children, beloved of the people. They are the next generation of leaders that observers are curious about. They are social figures, granting mere mortals the closest glimpse into what royal life is like. They are not your grandparents' kings and queens. We have enjoyed greater access to William and Harry.

William, the eldest, is to succeed his father, now King Charles III of England, to the throne. His entire life has been in preparation for that predestined reality. His younger brother, Harry, as the second son, has the option to abdicate both his royal title and access to public funding. His birthright was to succeed his father to the throne should his brother die prematurely, yet he can also choose not to serve his country at all without experiencing the same level of public scrutiny William might receive if he simply chose not to be king. In a manner of speaking, Prince William takes on the duties of succession by being the firstborn of the former Prince and Princess of Wales, to whom he holds his current title, while Harry reaps the benefits of a royal upbringing without being beholden to continue to serve the crown. This is a unique analogy, but it paints the picture of what Christ did for the family of believers, by bearing a burden we reap the benefit of. That is the crux of the geographical advantage provided by being in Jesus's bloodline.

The scriptures tell us that Jesus is seated at the right hand of the Father (Colossians 3:1; Romans 8:34; Ephesians 2:6). Christ's cypher or royal mark is indicative of His unquestionable authority. He rules and reigns, one biblical scholar said, from a seated position of rest because the work He did is finished, completed on our behalf. The blood of Jesus embodied in His covenant of grace grants believers, His set-apart ones, a royal inheritance that transcends geography and location.

Where you are, Christ is also (Joshua 1:9). There is no depth His love cannot reach nor mountain that can keep Him from you (Matthew 17:14–21). Romans 8:29 shares that we are more than conquerors because He has conquered in our stead and gone ahead of us (Isaiah 45). Again and again, the scriptures plainly state in that same prayer found in the Gospel of John that we are one as

He is one with the Father, meaning no matter where we are, we have full access to the rights and privilege His blood shed for us to have, which are the rights of citizenship in heaven. This privilege can manifest as not only rights to commune with God in prayer at will, but it also leads to access to healing, financial recourse, divine support, supernatural powers, and authority to rule and reign with Him (Mark 9:23). Our rebirth into the kingdom of heaven allows us to choose to walk in the role of Prince William, heir apparent, or Prince Harry, royal affiliation without full title or benefits. The choice is ours. That means that geography is not a determining factor that can hinder us. We are advantaged to be here on earth while a place has been secured for us in heaven. The Word of God reminds us that even while our geography is on earth, we are partakers of the heavenly vision (Acts 2; John 3). Ephesians 1:3 (AMP) reads, "Blessed *and* worthy of praise be the God and Father of our Lord Jesus Christ, who has blessed us with every spiritual blessing in the heavenly realms in Christ." "Realm" is a geography term explaining the location to which we have access. Later in the book, we read that "through the church the multifaceted wisdom of God [in all its countless aspects] might now be made known [revealing the mystery] to the [angelic] rulers and authorities in the heavenly places" (Ephesians 3:10, AMP). This was made possible by our proximity, or relationship, with Christ that removed the boundary between us and the things of heaven.

Deuteronomy 28 spells it out: we are blessed (or have the right to command the blessing) in our basket or kneading bowl, when we come in or go out, in our storehouses, in the land, and in all that we undertake. Even the offspring of our body (children) and what we can produce with our hands fall under the authority of the blessing because the Lord has commanded and insured it in blood. To sum it up, no matter where, God has got us.

TWO
CHALLENGING FEAR AND UNDERSTANDING IDENTITY

Reverend Billy Graham, a man who began his worldwide ministry humbly in the late 1930s at Florida Bible Institute, once said, "*Anxiety is the natural result when our hopes are centered in anything short of God and His will for us.*" Like Graham suggests, and Scripture confirms, fear comes in when we take our eyes off God. One of the most famous biblical narratives concerning fears that take us off course can be found in the story of Peter's walk on the water. Recalling the story told in the New Testament book of Matthew 14, we learn that, along with the other disciples, Peter had just witnessed the miraculous. Jesus took five loaves of bread and two fish, broke them, and, along with a crowd of several thousand, saw the food multiplied in the hands of His disciples.

Oftentimes, we hear a Bible story like this and find ourselves in a moment of awe. The creative miracle that took place is one we can doubt, marvel in, and regard, but we would be hard-pressed to fully comprehend the magnitude of the moment there on the grass with the multitude. These followers were content to push back the plate in order to hear what Jesus wanted to share. In fact, it is more likely that their bodily functions, the need to eat, drink, defecate, and micturate, were suspended while they basked in the glory. They followed Him from neighboring towns. Their sick were getting healed. The Word of God came forth from God in the flesh.

Their world had been turned upside down a bit. John the Baptist had been beheaded after spending nearly two years in jail and was now buried by his own disciples. The territory was controlled by Herod Antipas, who inherited the land from his father, Roman Emperor Herod the Great, and ruled from Galilee to Northern Palestine and the areas of Greece east of the Jordan River. Herod's reputation was one of political competence and sexual compromise. Yet Herod's successor, Caligula, had a far worse reputation. In short, the times in which this story took place were perilous for believers. Simon Peter would have been wary of nightfall as well as the sheer number of people when he and the others approached Jesus to have the crowds dismissed. All of this sets the stage for later that evening when both Jesus and Peter walked on the Sea of Galilee.

As much as we, modern believers, can still find awe in this narrative, we also dismiss it as out-of-date because we do not see the kinds of miracles Jesus said we would. Greater things than this, Jesus said, we would do. Yet where are these creative miracles? Where is the walking on water? Where is the wealth transfer we have long heard predicted? Let me clarify briefly before we continue: many of these things are happening and have happened, but the occurrences are so few and far between that we unintentionally do not expect to see the miraculous. We're still waiting for the big show. Nevertheless, if we understand who we are in Christ, our true identity, we'd be more apt to challenge fear and walk in the fullness of God's glory, miracles, and all.

There is a current debate over identity that can make life challenging for families, and it stems from perception rather than reality. Our self-perception can differ from our physical appearance and known characteristics that are widely accepted by society, a phase that happens to most people at some point during human growth and development. However, for some, the obsession with making self-perception and physical appearance match can lead to costly surgery, years of therapy, and denial of the true self. Denial of the true self is a win for our enemy because we are made to be image-bearers of God Himself. Genesis records the conversation the Triune God had regarding our rulership, likeness, and blessing. Male and female, He made us, to intentionally rule over and take dominion in the land. The divine design concerning us was and remains a perpetual duty to subdue earth. Without identity, it is difficult to rule over the weeds in our backyard, let alone anything of substance. That is partially why I have written this book.

I shared with you about the miracles I participated in regarding my own health, but another part of my life's struggle has been managing the fear I often felt. Identity starts with belonging. Researchers have aptly concluded and poured millions of dollars into understanding how to help children feel a sense of belonging in school to help curb childhood suicide. Psychologists define "belonging" as a human emotional need to affiliate with and be accepted by members of a group. Belonging does not rely on proximity but rather comes from the perception of quality, meaning, and satisfaction with social connections. These definitions often reference the historical marginalization of women, certain religious factions, ethnic minorities, and, more commonly now, those in certain affinity groups of sexual identity and sexual expression. Yet, if we return to Genesis, we see clearly that we were designed with belonging in mind. He who created all things created us for the purpose of dominion, and we belong not only to God's family but also to His purpose and plans. In other words, we belong in a deeper way to Christ than we ever could with another person, organization, or entity. When we do not reciprocate God's offer of belonging, we will undoubtedly find ourselves settling for an identity that is less than our true self.

When I started kindergarten, I was told by the leading group of students I encountered that I did not belong. The school year was in full swing by the time my parents decided to enroll me in public school. Previously, I spent some time in a Montessori school, which failed to prepare me for walking onto the oversized campus with my father back in the time when parents could still walk their children to class. We lived in Phoenix at that time, a predominantly White suburban area despite the state's Spanish history. Even though I was a mere five-year-old, I understood immediately that there was a difference between the other students and me. They made sure of it. But my teacher came to my rescue and told me I belonged. She silenced the sneers and jeers to my salvation. Hers was the first effort I recall in making sure I felt as if I belonged.

The human mind is funny. I felt that I belonged in a classroom because of that kindergarten teacher—even though I can't say I enjoyed school terribly much, I would remain in a classroom setting as both pupil and teacher for the next forty years. My parents, by their own mouths, would say that their divorce was an ugly one. Prior to their separation, my brother and I were living in the midst of a storm, a storm of partying, fighting, drinking, drugging, and perversion. While I tried to fit into that world, it was obvious that I could not. So, I clung to my brother until I could find belonging of my own. As it happened, my kindergarten teacher gave me a semblance of belonging, but it was short-lived, and fear set in.

Fear meditated upon can take us from God.

There are many names for the God of Abraham, Isaac, and Jacob, the God of Israel. The Old Testament book of Isaiah 41:8–10 calls God the Helper of Israel, and it is in this chapter that we find a command from God about fear.

> But you, Israel, are my servant.
>
> You're Jacob, my first choice,
>
> descendants of my good friend Abraham.
>
> I pulled you in from all over the world,
>
> called you in from every dark corner of the earth,
>
> Telling you, "You're my servant, serving on my side.
>
> I've picked you. I haven't dropped you."
>
> Don't panic. I'm with you.
>
> There's no need to fear for I'm your God.
>
> I'll give you strength. I'll help you.
>
> I'll hold you steady, keep a firm grip on you.
>
> Isaiah 41:8–10 (MSG)

One hundred forty-five times, the Bible says, "Fear not." Could it be that there is a reason not to fear that is exceedingly more significant than the temporary enemy we face?

Most people face fear in their daily life. But the way our brains respond to fear can be a pathway to making decrees and allegiances that take us off course when it comes to a faith walk with God, therefore changing how we perceive our identity. The part of our brain that controls impulses is activated when we fear, slowing down other brain processes. The emotional experience processed in our frontal lobe can elicit one of four fear responses designed to "keep us safe" from the fear-causing threat: fight, flight, freeze, or fawn.

It will be more likely that you have heard of the first three fear responses but to quickly review, understand this: anger at the fear elicits a fight response, fear of danger often results in the flight response, and anxiety-provoking situations create the freeze response. Our brain analyzes the situation quickly and makes an impromptu response, often without our conscious participation. Younger people often are not even aware that a brain decision has been made. They mentally "find" themselves hiding as they are discovered by a caregiver. Those who freeze might experience momentary muteness, unable to even explain what happened to cause them to fear. Those who answer fear with a fight response zone in on defeating their enemy in a kind of tunnel vision, to the exclusion of all else. In our world today, however, the fawn response is becoming more and more prevalent. Fawning is often a response to trauma when the brain decides to try and please whoever is triggering the fear response to prevent them from causing harm. It may manifest as compliance, which should not be confused with consent, as the brain is simply looking to provide a survival option. We see fawning in the form of a spouse staying in an abusive marriage, the Stockholm syndrome with the victims of kidnapping, the way a sexual abuse victim excuses the actions of the perpetrator of the crimes against them, and other extreme forms of harm-inducing fear scenarios.

All of these fear responses exist outside of the will of Jesus Christ. His death and sacrifice are why the Word of God can say "Fear not" as often as it does. Because Christ's finished work means we as believers can have a different response to frightful situations: authority. We have the authority and right to plead the blood of Jesus over a situation that can overcome our brain's desire to fight, fear, freeze, or fawn. In fact, it is a different kind of fight response, a spiritual response to warfare. Ephesians 6:12 (AMP) says, "For our struggle is not against flesh and blood [contending only with physical opponents], but against the rulers, against the powers, against the world forces of this [present] darkness, against the spiritual *forces* of wickedness in the heavenly (supernatural) *places*." The blood of Jesus is more than enough to fight for us. If stolen or forgotten identity and fear kept us from dwelling in His presence in the fullness to which He has called us, then it is His good pleasure to defeat it. The blood is our shield and our shelter, our defense against any enemy. For that, we must be truly grateful, for it is the blood of Jesus and the grace of God that perfects our weakness. God does not leave us without options.

As we deal with fear, we have an opportunity to annul the agreements we made in the moment we looked at the situations in our lives instead of looking at God. Let's face the fact that human frailty will cause us to speak out of the wrong side of our mouths when faced with a fearful situation. We've agreed with the enemy when it was spoken of us, "You're not good enough." We've uttered our own condemnations and spoken those ills over others. We have even sabotaged ourselves with our deeds. Sometimes, we buckle under the weight of sin, shame, and guilt. But God has a better way. We cannot waste the grace available to us through the blood of Jesus. And as the blood grants us access to the courts of heaven, isn't it time we as a people annul the words spoken over us that are in direct contradiction to what God says about us? It is a matter of identity. If we be in Christ and He in us, let us come boldly to the throne of grace and be made whole.

I previously mentioned that I found belonging in a classroom. After that kindergarten experience, my family moved to Georgia. Instead of being the only person of color in the room (as I was in Arizona), I became the only outsider of a different sort. I knew nothing of my Black heritage. I knew nothing of hopscotch, Now and Later candy, and cornrows. I stood out in a classroom of my peers like a sore thumb and was persecuted for it. The glimpse of belonging I felt at the age of five was so far in the rearview when I entered the school that stood three stories high, between two ghettos, in downtown Atlanta. I was engulfed in fear and wanted out. After a failed attempted suicide in fifth grade, I "fawned" my way into a solution by agreeing with the enemy about who I was and whose I was. That is exactly how people miss the destiny God has called us into. We make the attack about us instead of about the Word of God. So, it is time that we as a body annul those words and agreements that we spoke in a moment of fear and lost identity.

We have to realize that today is the acceptable time for grace to reign, for identity to be restored, and for fear to be forever defeated. Our Father is looking for a people to worship Him in spirit and truth—this does not occur when we bow to our fears or, worse, do not know who we belong to in the kingdom. For us to really be free to worship God as He deserves, we have to know who we are in relationship to Him. This is essential to knowing our identity in Christ.

When approaching the throne room to annul the words we have spoken or to ask that words spoken over us be annulled, it is prudent to understand the spirit behind the words. I recently read a short book by Mary Garrison (2014) for some reference material to support these spiritual legal proceedings. Garrison identified ten spiritual strongholds that can come by a word of agreement. Amongst them is fear, which is where we will focus. But it is important for your future study of the Word of God and wholeness that you recognize the other spirits that can manifest rotten fruit in our lives.

The spirits of bondage, jealousy, perversion, haughtiness, and other Antichrist spirits manifest in us as an opposition to Christ's design for our lives. The spirit of bondage manifests as anguish, bitterness, addiction, oppression, brokenness, ambition, lust, compulsory sin, avarice, or compulsory subjection. The spirit of heaviness is represented by mourning, grief, sorrow, despair, hopelessness, loneliness, discouragement, rejection, self-pity, gluttony, and gloominess. The spirit of jealousy manifests as murder, anger, wrath, revenge, spite, cruelty, hate, rage, suspicion, covetousness, competition, rivalry, discord and dissention, and selfishness. The spirit of perversion manifests as wounding, snares, hatred, foolishness, despicableness, lust, fretfulness, rebellion, sexual perversion, inordinate love of self, false teaching, and perversion of truth. The familiar and divination spirits manifest as witches, wizards, hypnotists, clairvoyants, necromancers, conjurers, enchanters, soothsayers, stargazers, belomancers, splanchomancers, teraphims, ventriloquists, voyeurs, and mutters. The spirit of whoredoms manifests as harlotry and idolatry of any kind. The spirit of haughtiness manifests as pride, scorn, mockery, lofty looks, bragging, stiff-neckedness, wrath, gossip, contention, egoism, self-righteousness, exalted feelings, vanity, arrogance, dictatorialness, insolence, self-assertion, and holier-than-thou attitudes. The lying spirit manifests as strong delusions, insinuation, exaggeration, flattery, vain babbling, condemning, profanity, hypocrisy, religiousness, frenzied emotional responses, driving zeal, superstitions, and vain imagination. Finally, the Antichrist spirit is any spirit in opposition to Christ, His doctrine, humanity, deity, or victory on the cross. Antichrist spirits operate on the earth today and often claim substitute methods of atoning for sin or claims of ultimate or "other" authorities, which bind people to church law rather than Scripture. Garrison goes on to say that opposition to the prophetical office, attacks on individuals' personal testimonies, blasphemies, persecution of the saints, seducing believers into error, and attempts to thwart God's millennial plan are all Antichrist in nature.

The spirit of fear, which we are focused on for the purpose of annulling words of agreement, may manifest in our lives in many ways beyond simple timidity. Fear can range from one end of the spectrum to the other, from fright (Psalm 55:5) to terror (Deuteronomy 32:25; Isaiah 54:14). Other manifestations include shyness, worry, feelings of inadequacy, tension (stress), phobias, hypercriticism, perfectionism and introversion. With prolonged fear, there is always a potential for the person to become demented. Manifestations of paranoia, schizophrenia, delusions of grandeur, insanity, melancholia, and bipolar disorder can come when one submits to the spirit of fear, although these manifestations are exhibitions of the deaf and dumb spirit.

David prayed about fear in many of the psalms, and with great reason. He was targeted not only by his father-in-law, King Saul, but he was also the target of scorn by his brothers, father, and wife, not to mention all the enemies of Israel he encountered when he served as king. In one scripture, David petitions, "Lord, do not ignore my plea" (Psalm 55:1, HCSB). We have already read that the term "plea" is a legal term in which an action is generated by a judge when the action has been submitted in accordance with the court's protocols. This is our part to engage in. When we plea our case to the Just Judge, in this case, to ask for an annulment of the words of agreement, we must enter that petition correctly.

In Christ, we have life, love, truth, righteousness, peace, hope, goodness, freedom, mercy, compassion, forgiveness, justice, power, healing, knowledge, wisdom, reconciliation, and authority. The opposite of those is found in a life without Christ and includes everything from fear and deception to deterioration and chaos. To progress from the lowest recesses of humanity to the speed of Mach 1 spiritually, we must shed light on the misconceptions or lies we have agreed with in moments of fear.

First, let us be reminded that becoming a Christian is a personal choice. In doing so, we must recognize that this personal choice has benefits that come with the decision to accept Christ as

Lord and Savior; among those benefits is access to heaven. Next, let us be reminded that salvation cannot be earned. You may ask yourself what salvation has to do with the courts of heaven. To that, I respond, "Absolutely everything." The gift of salvation is given exclusively by God through Jesus. Knowing that we have accepted a gift through Jesus from Creator God ought to give us a little bit of confidence as we approach the heavenly courtroom. Amen.

Another misconception is that we as believers have been commissioned, that is, certified, sanctioned, and licensed in an official capacity, to go into all the world with the gospel of Jesus. Sometimes, when we hear "go into all the world," we do not take it seriously or literally. We think our mission field is relegated to our family alone. Sometimes, we start considering *our world* instead of the world. The Word says we can do all things through Christ, who strengthens us. Do we actually imagine the strength of Christ can only handle our messed-up selves or our messed-up family? God can do exceedingly, abundantly above all. That means He can license us to walk in faith. He can sanction us to take dominion for Christ in the more remote parts of the world. We can be sanctioned to leave the shackles of fear behind and walk upright in the newness of life. This is how we walk in our commission, knowing that according to Jesus's own words in Mark 9:23 (CSB), "Everything is possible for him who believes." It's official! Jesus Himself said it...those who believe are overcomers.

We overcome fear, unbelief, and lack of identity through Christ. But if our words have betrayed us by agreeing with the enemy, we must petition the courts to have our words annulled. What does "to be annulled" mean? Canceled out, nullified, to be voided; no longer law. In other words, when a decision or a word has been annulled, it is obliterated and invalidated. Most commonly, we hear the word "annulment" used in special cases of divorce in which the marriage is deemed to have never happened by a judge. An annulment is possible only if there is a specific reason why your marriage was never legally valid. The reason for voiding your marriage is the grounds for annulment. Anyone can get a no-fault divorce if both parties want a marriage to come to an end. However, an annulment resolves that there is no marriage once the grounds have been satisfied in court to end the union. These include fraud, duress, underage, incest, polygamy, concealment, and failed consummation. Spiritually speaking, using our words to agree with the enemy is a similar type of fraud that gives us, as believers, grounds for divorce from those words. We can annul the impact of the agreement and renew our minds to the business at hand—serving God in the freedom of true identity. Before approaching God's courtroom for an annulment of the words of agreement, we must renew our minds to the mission set before us. Picture it this way: say you have agreed with the enemy about your own self-worth. It has led you to a life of defeat and self-doubt. Petitioning God's courtroom for an annulment of the agreement is ineffective and futile because we haven't changed our self-talk.

Long before I knew anything about the courts of heaven, I was praying about a friend's self-talk. The person was always so negative and skeptical of any new idea. They often rained on my parade when I shared what God was doing in my life. Our relationship strained over the years because she was just no fun to be around. Spiritually, she was a buzz kill. I wanted to maintain the relationship but understood if things remained as they currently were, I would spend all my time processing feelings and forgiving the offense I would naturally feel when she spewed negativity. I sought the Lord, and the Holy Spirit used something in nature to illustrate the spiritual condition my friend was operating in.

It was a spring day, and we were on a road trip going south. Along the highway, I kept seeing tall weeds that had grown through the cracks in the concrete in the median. Each was two to three feet in height, which is tall for a weed, but that is where the plant stalled. Some of the weeds might have been trees springing up or some other plant. Regardless of the kind of plant, none were taller than three feet in height because there was no soil for them to continue to grow. They were surrounded by concrete—the plant itself was choked. The Holy Spirit said that is how negative words impact our spiritual growth. We can speak the Word according to godliness, but when we agree with the enemy, we choke out the good words, and they can only produce small growth. We will never grow in godliness if we speak with a loose tongue that has both good and evil coming from it. In other words, we cannot annul words we still agree with. We must find healing in the knowledge of who we are in Christ. Then and only then can we annul words of agreement spoken by us in fear and ignorance. Let me be clear. We cannot annul that which we are actively doing. When you know, through the wisdom of the Holy Spirit, that there is a word of agreement working against you, then you can petition the courtroom of heaven for an annulment of the words of agreement.

Let me give you a practical example from my own life. I moved in with a friend I had known for twenty years after a long separation between us. God brought us together again for a reason unknown to me at the time. Within days of moving in, things started to break around the house. First, it was a GFCI outlet that blew when I plugged in a coffee maker. That 300-dollar unexpected expense was something neither of us was excited about. Next, a ceiling fan motor went out. Then, she broke the handle on the refrigerator. She noticed that the blender was not performing as it had when I began to use it. The microwave suddenly stopped working, and there was a problem with the plumbing. Now we were in a well-maintained 700-thousand-dollar home. There was no explanation for why things suddenly started breaking around the house. Aside from the coffee maker and blender, I had not even touched the items that broke, but she was convinced I brought a "broke" spirit into the home that was wreaking havoc with her appliances.

I believe the truth of the matter is that she had assigned a broke spirit to me in her mind. Add to that the desperation she was dealing with as a result of her marriage failing and the sudden loss of her job. She felt broken, as anyone would in that situation.

But being people of faith, we joined in prayer against the spirit of brokenness. Both of us had been taught in church not to say "I'm broke" when referring to our finances, a teaching she took to heart with religiosity. While I was intentional about the new habit, I did not take it to her level. What she hadn't considered is the other ways that people can be broken. Ultimately, I believe the enemy wanted me removed from her home so that he could capitalize on her hurt and drive her from God for good (she had already stopped going to church out of embarrassment and hurt over the failure of her marriage). Once I recognized her stress and the opportunity the enemy attempted to create, by revelation of God, I prayed not only for an annulment of broken words but of the broken spirit. That Rhema Word from God directed my prayer and gave me access to the courtroom to petition for a legal judgment in my favor.

With regard to the manifestation of our annulment of agreement regarding brokenness, I don't think that my friend won't ever have another broken appliance. In this case, broken blenders and ceiling fans were not her real problem. The problem is any place that opens a foothold to the enemy to take away identity. Hers was the rejection she felt when her husband walked out, and she got laid off from her job soon thereafter. She, like so many of us, even myself, years prior, took our identity in our title, our offices, our marriages, and other accolades instead of in Christ, the author and finisher of our faith. After our shared prayer, I retreated to pray in secret concerning brokenness and continued to live a life of faith in front of her.

When we spoke about her situation, and I'd offer advice, she would remark, "You're ten years on the other side of these feelings. It just happened to me, and I don't know what to do."

My heart went out to her. At the time, I had been divorced for thirteen years and was truly living my best life. But it hadn't happened overnight. I went through the rejection and grief of divorce like anyone else. One difference in the way the two of us handled the months following the abandonment of our husbands was that I went all in when it came to a life with God while she secluded herself from the community of faith. I believe God reconnected us at this time so she would have her own community of faith in the home since she was not comfortable leaving home in her grief. The enemy brought brokenness to scare her from being in fellowship with me again after all these years. But God.

We, as believers, must release ourselves from the versions of ourselves we created to survive. We must release ourselves from permanent decisions made about temporary situations. Perhaps you have been hurt by a spouse and then vowed in your heart never to trust again. Those words must be annulled. Maybe you found yourself in a fearful situation and chose to shelter yourself from living a full life in response. Annul that fear and the covenant you made with it. Did someone say that because of your gender, ethnicity, or socio-economic standing, you can't do or go somewhere, and, in your heart, you agreed? Annul that agreement because it is against your God-identity. When we are immature believers, deceived by fear or temporarily hindered by pain, we tend to look with the natural eye instead of our spiritual ones. In these moments, our mouths speak from the abundance of our hearts, which are situation and circumstance-focused instead of being laser-focused on God's providence. The words God speaks of us in His Word and in our hearts are infinitely truer than any temporary emotion we may be feeling. While most believers understand these concepts in our heads, we have failed to annul the words of agreement we spoke in response. You may say, "I have never spoken words against my identity to anyone, yet I am still experiencing the effects of wrong covenants with circumstance." Recognize that what we believe in our hearts about ourselves can still shape our future even if we have never told a soul how we feel. Our actions show the true feelings we may not have even admitted to ourselves. That is why we need the Holy Spirit to reveal the ways in which we have agreed with our enemy, our situation, our pain, or our fear.

Pray in the name of Jesus that the Lord of all the earth reveals the ways in which we have spoken words, either aloud or in our hearts, that need to be annulled. Look for patterns in your life that you want removed. For example, do you always seek out the same type of partner only to wonder why you attract that kind of man or woman when the relationship ends horribly? Annul any words of agreement that say that you do not deserve better. Do you settle for being overlooked at work when you deserve a promotion? Annul any words of agreement that say it's not your time for promotion. Are you malcontent with any part of your life? Pray that the Lord reveals ways in which you have a wrong understanding of your role, your purpose, and His plan for you. Then, seek an audience with the Just Judge regarding your annulment. These actions set us up in a position for God to act. Because as a person of free will, He will not violate your own confession. Rather, He provides grace until that self-talk is changed.

As you pray based on the revealed Word of God to your heart, sincerely understand that an annulment means it (whatever you agreed with) never happened. The covenant will be erased from the heavenly record. God will forget it, and so should you. You must be prepared to change your self-talk, so practice new self-talk even before you pray and show yourself that you can be disciplined enough to take back your identity in Christ. Be fearless when you pray, knowing that this petition is not only biblical but also God's desire for you to be free from fear and words of agreement that are contrary to God's Word. Jesus said, "I say only what the Father who sent me has told me to say" (John 12:49, CEV). The just shall live by faith (Romans 1:12, Galatians 3:11; Hebrews 10:38). We are not justified by the law but by our faith in Jesus Christ. Re-read the scriptures referenced above and mutter them in your heart. This primes the soil of your heart to receive deliverance from fear and the words of agreement you spoke in fear. Be set free!

THREE

THE ROAD TO PURPOSE: ABOUT YOUR AUTHORITY

Even before we think about our authority as Christian believers, we must fully understand from whom that authority comes: Jesus. Let us also take note that the road to purpose is a long one. It's a marathon, not a sprint. We go from glory to glory in Christ (2 Corinthians 3:18), which means that we never stop pursuing purpose when we walk in God's authority. I have been pursuing purpose for decades before I hit the tip of the iceberg when it comes to understanding God's divine design for mankind. Of course, I could read and understand on a surface level, but it clicked in my heart only after a long time of study and seeking God. This is not meant to discourage anyone from pressing toward the high calling. It should excite us to know that there is always more in God. We cannot get to the end of Him because His nature is creative. It is our great pleasure to be given a new experience in God daily as we seek Him. I am convinced that the reason the universe is still expanding today is because God has something more to show us. Like any good father, He wraps purpose as a present. He produces opportunities for us to shine in purpose. His is the pleasure we find when we walk with Him in covenant, and we receive the benefit of purpose.

Perhaps you have studied authority before. Good, keep studying. Let us commit ourselves to walk in the fullness of authority on the earth so that we can prepare for the marriage supper of the Lamb. In other words, for as much as we talk about Jesus coming back, have we considered how ill-prepared we are to receive Him? Remember the dream I shared about going to a wedding shoeless? That is the body of Christ right now. We're clothed in the full armor of God, ready for the wedding, yet we are spiritually shoeless when it comes to going into all the world and bringing guests to this grand event. A wedding without guests is an elopement, and I genuinely doubt God waited all this time just to run off to Vegas for a midnight nuptial at a roadside chapel. No, I suggest He is planning a royal affair. His return and our union with Him is an event He has delayed in hopes of bringing more people to this kingdom covenant. Ours is the authority to walk on this earth, taking back cities, households, schools, government, media, medicine, and religion. Yes, I said religion as well.

These are sometimes called the seven mountains of influence. Each of these areas of authority should be managed by Spirit-filled believers. Then and only then will we have fully walked in the fullness of our authority. Why do I believe this so fervently? First of all, the Word of God says as much. Let's begin with the authority we have over our own person. Colossians Chapter Three is subtitled "Rules for Holy Living." This is as good a place to start as any. While I suggest studying the chapter in its entirety in your free time, let's look at verses one through ten for a brief summary of the ways in which we can take authority over our flesh in this season of life. Here is the version in The Message Translation so you do not have to look it up, but I encourage you to compare it to the translation you prefer in order to have a greater understanding of God's Word:

> So, if you're serious about living this new resurrection life with Christ, *act* like it. Pursue the things over which Christ presides. Don't shuffle along, eyes to the ground, absorbed with the things right in front of you. Look up and be alert to what is going on around Christ—that's where the action is. See things from *his* perspective.

> Your old life is dead. Your new life, which is your *real* life—even though invisible to spectators—is with Christ in God. *He* is your life. When Christ (your real life, remember) shows up again on this earth, you'll show up, too—

the real you, the glorious you. Meanwhile, be content with obscurity, like Christ.

And that means killing off everything connected with that way of death: sexual promiscuity, impurity, lust, doing whatever you feel like whenever you feel like it, and grabbing whatever attracts your fancy. That's a life shaped by things and feelings instead of by God. It's because of this kind of thing that God is about to explode in anger. It wasn't long ago that you were doing all that stuff and not knowing any better. But you know better now, so make sure it's all gone for good: bad temper, irritability, meanness, profanity, dirty talk.

Don't lie to one another. You're done with that old life. It's like a filthy set of ill-fitting clothes you've stripped off and put in the fire. Now you're dressed in a new wardrobe. Every item of your new way of life is custom-made by the Creator, with his label on it. All the old fashions are now obsolete. Words like Jewish and non-Jewish, religious, and irreligious, insider and outsider, uncivilized and uncouth, slave and free, mean nothing. From now on everyone is defined by Christ, everyone is included in Christ.

Colossians 3:1–10 (MSG)

"Act like it," the Word says. The church as a whole has a lot of problems listed here in Paul's letter to the believers in Colosse. At the time of this writing, the city was experiencing a decline even though it was perched high on a ridge in modern Turkey. It was a major trade route in Asia Minor and the people there were known for the dark red wool cloth they produced. Colosse was a Roman province, so Paul would have been free to travel there; however, the letter was written during Paul's first imprisonment, shortly after AD 60. Despite some false teaching and heresy that found its way into the Colossian church, Paul reminds the believers that all authority was given to Him, Jesus, who is a joint heir with us (Colossians 1:9–2:19). However, he encouraged them to put to death their old, fleshly ways in order to be alive through the Spirit of God.

It is important to understand that there are people who will end up in heaven even though they never experienced being alive. Consider the criminal who was saved on the cross with Jesus moments before their earthly deaths. No one would say he had any evidence of being alive through the Spirit of God except the words Jesus spoke. Death bed conversions are better than no conversion at all—if you have a family member far from Christ, you'll take it. But God prefers and even designed opportunities for us to walk out our salvation with fear and trembling of the authority He gave through Christ. We have a purpose, and it is not just to get to heaven. Our goal must be to be a witness of God's greatness here on earth—to have a ministry as Jesus did before reaching our Father in heaven. But if we operate outside of our authority, in the flesh, or in doublemindedness, we do Jesus's cross no honor. As one preacher said, we cannot waste our grace.

I don't know if I've written about this before, but it bears repeating because only this year did I get the full understanding of what God meant by this word of knowledge. A decade ago, in 2013, Paul Crouch died. He was the co-founder of Trinity Broadcasting Network (TBN) with his wife, Jan. At the time, TBN reached every major continent via eighty-four satellites and over 18,000 affiliates. My mother and I had been watching TBN that day; various programs ran in the background throughout the day. It was the week of Thanksgiving, and there had been a lot of activity in the house. That evening, when we finally sat back down in front of the television, we saw the news of Dr. Crouch's passing. Like the rest of the world, we were shocked and saddened by the loss to Christian broadcasting. Of course, there was concern over Dr. Crouch's longtime co-host and closest friend. *How would she manage?* I remember asking myself. As we sat there in silence, I heard the voice of the Holy Spirit in my heart. He said, "Paul Crouch is dead. Run with it."

The first thing that came to my mind after hearing from God was the scripture found in Joshua 21.

"Moses my servant is dead. Now then, you and all these people, get ready to cross the Jordan River into the land I am about to give to them—to the Israelites" (Joshua 1:2, NIV).

Now, I've always been a writer (and a runner, for that matter). Over the years, I began writing screenplays for Christian television. God helped me to understand that to reach all people, we must utilize technology and media. That was something the Crouchs understood. As a child, my mother partnered with both TBN and PTL dutifully. I grew up watching these two pioneers on television. At this moment, God revealed to my heart that there is more work to be done for the kingdom. But what my role might be, I was unsure. Even though I knew very well the path these leaders took to build the largest Christian broadcasting network, I had no wherewithal in the natural to run with anything. I simply pondered these things in my heart, perhaps as Mary did, when the Spirit spoke to me things I did not understand. This year, a decade later, I began to understand more of what God meant when He spoke to me that night.

Our purpose as Christians is directly tied to our authority in heaven. In other words, when the Word says, "What we bind on earth is bound in heaven and what we loose on earth is loosed in heaven" (Matthew 18:18, NIV), it speaks of authority. Another way of saying it is that we, as believers, must improve our God IQ.

Let me tell you what I mean by that. IQ, or intelligence quotient—the measure of your knowledge—is based on not just ability but the ability to discipline yourself enough for that ability to come forth and impact the surroundings. We all lack discipline in one area or another. That is not the focus today. In order to improve our God IQ, we must inquire of the Lord the things we are given ability in and can be disciplined enough to bring forth. Without a vision, the people perish. Many of us are perishing even in our faith because we do not share the vision of what God has called us to. Dr. Myles Monroe says, "When we capture a vision, it simplifies everything. Because vision controls all of your choices after that." The Bible supports this notion when it says that discipline comes from vision.

When I was a freshman in college (for the second time), my writing professor told me that writers write every day. I considered myself a writer and was passionate about it. Despite that passion and perceived ability, I went through seasons of life when I never picked up a pen or sat down at a computer to write. When I was raising young children, I didn't write. Even though children offer a wealth of story ideas every time they say the darndest things. But vision comes from God. Once I turned my pen toward God, the habit of writing every day became an easy, if not an insatiable, practice. In fact, I became a teacher so that I would have more time to write. Editing is not my calling, but it is part of the writing process. I had to discipline myself to value editing and participate in that part of the process. Publishing was not important to me when I first began writing. Over the years, the need to share my writing with the world has snowballed. I became disciplined enough to recognize that what God gave me to write about was for more than just my amusement and knowledge.

This came to a head the day I was on my way to church with a recent publication that I planned on giving to my pastor's wife and his mother. I had five preview copies of this book I thought the church should purchase for our women's conference. My plan was to give the books as gifts. The sheer brilliance of the words would do the rest, I imagined. But when I stepped into the ladies' room before taking my seat, the Lord told me to give one of the two books to the cleaning woman who took care of our facilities. I didn't even know if this woman was a believer, or reader, or anything about her, except that she kept our bathrooms clean. But I had learned the hard way to be obedient with my writing. I gave her the book, she thanked me, and I headed into the sanctuary looking for the pastor's mother, Sister Katie Franklin. Before I got to the section where she normally sat, I heard the Lord speak again. He told me to give the other book to the surrogate who would be preaching that day. It was the first service, and although I hesitated to be obedient this time around, I knew I had two more books in the car and could give those to the ladies during the second service if I really wanted to. I knew Dr. Rutland would be making his way down the aisles greeting people before church. I found him easily, gave him the book, and walked away with a fake smile on my face.

I had five copies of this book I thought was very powerful, and I coveted those to whom I planned on giving them. The writing was perfect for a female readership, and that's why I wanted the head ladies in our church to have them. Here, I was tasked with giving one book to the cleaning lady and another to Dr. Mark Rutland in the pulpit, who would probably dismiss it as too elementary. I was working the main cameras as part of our production team, and it was time for me to take my place for service. After sulking a bit more, I asked God why He had me give the books in the manner He did instead of what I planned. He plainly stated, "I wanted to show you that those words are from everyone...from the Ph.D. to the cleaning crew."

I had it in my head that my audience for that particular book was middle-aged moms and wives. And no one else. I didn't even realize the power of the message God gave me. My vision was smaller than God's when it came to that book.

There's something we need to know about vision. Oftentimes, we see parts and not the whole. Dr. Myles Monroe shared another important fact about vision. He said,

- "Vision will choose your future."

- "Vision will choose your friends."

- "Vision will choose your library."

- "Vision will choose your use of time."

- "Vision will choose your use of energy."

- "Vision will choose your priorities in life."

- "Vision will even choose your hobbies."

- "Vision chooses how you spend your money, your attitude, lifestyle, your values, how to plan, your behavior, and the list goes on and on."

Basically, vision will dictate every aspect of life because even the games you play and the movies you watch will be related to vision if you can only catch it. People often say that what aggravates you about the world is your calling, the thing you have been called to change. I disagree that there is a higher vision that the calling must fulfill. I know I am called to work with rescuing trafficked persons or those at risk for trafficking. But the vision God has placed in my heart is actually more vast than that. You might scoff, "What can be bigger than the trafficking industry?" I'd scoff, too. In fact, I did. Then, I believed.

Trafficking is one boulder in the mountain of government and family. As a result of the condition of man's heart and government regulation, hundreds of people are trafficked every day. If trafficking were abolished today, there would still be a problem in government and the condition of man's heart. That is why we, as believers, must understand authority enough to take back the mountains of influence as we prepare for Christ's return. I'm presenting a different way of looking at the problems we face globally. Hunger, sexual violence, corruption, bondages of all kinds, indoctrination, deception in medicine, and all kinds of unbelief are all boulders in these mountains of influence. If the church unified and said to these mountains, "Be thou removed," then and only then can we really say we are ready for the marriage supper of the Lamb.

This is not to say that the small steps each of us take in prayer, giving, and action are not beneficial. They are. Nevertheless, this world still needs to see a Bible-believing church take authority in the land and dominion in the name of Jesus.

So, what are the practical actions that lead to this spiritual dominion? I do not claim to be an authority on authority in Christ. But what I do know is that God left His Word for us to believe. If we believe, simply, the Word says, nothing is impossible for us (Mark 9:23).

The mountains of cultural influence are a concept that helps our minds categorize the areas of authority Jesus died and gave us the right to take dominion over. Leaders have vision, and it clarifies purpose.

THE FAMILY

God designed family in a hierarchical structure for the perpetuating of His kingdom in the universe, not just on earth. Family is the centerpiece not just of God's creation but of any functioning society. Divorce, fatherlessness, abuse, infidelity, and homosexuality are the primary disruptors of the family. When we see marriages fail at the rate they are in the United States and abroad, we can clearly understand there is a problem in the family. Now, the family is but one mountain, but the family connects and interacts with all other areas of cultural influence and, therefore, is connected to the other mountains. A moral foundation for the family is provided in Genesis and is further clarified throughout the Word of God. We cannot continue to see the family aborted due to trending movements, theories, and outside influences. The family is God's and God's alone. It must be run like God intended in order for it to operate in authority. If you are called to this mountain of authority, you will not only have a strong marriage (not perfect marriage) but a strong sense of family as well. Can a single person be called to "the family"? Yes. Singletons need authority and have a calling, just like married people. But it should be obvious that a person who has never been married or has only had failed marriages cannot hold the authority of the cultural mountain of family.

I, like many believers, am passionate about rebuilding the family. But until I have a strong marriage and get my own life together, I choose to sit down, listen, and learn. When we open our mouths, it should be because God tells us to. Let us stick to the mountain and boulders to which we have been called. All else, we can pray about. That being said, let God be true and all men a lie. If God told you to tackle the mountain of family, hopefully beginning with your own, let it be confirmed by two or three witnesses and go forth in God. Let no man tell you who God created you to be. That's His job. Not mine or anyone else's.

EDUCATION

Most of us acknowledge the mistake Western education made when they removed biblical principles and prayer from students' daily routines. As a teacher, I could go on and on about this stronghold. Children are some of the easiest targets in society. Regardless of your proclivities politically, we should all be able to agree that children should be protected, instructed, and morally trained in the ways that are most beneficial for living in godliness. That being said, restoring biblical truths and godly morality to our educational systems is crucial for the survival of our country, any country, for that matter. There is a biblical mandate for any nation under God to raise children in the way they should go, which was laid out through Jesus's ministry.

Now, to relate to my previous point about people with only failed marriages not leading the marriage conference, please remind yourself that as God in the flesh, Jesus was the ultimate teacher even though He did not have earthly children. Parenthood is not a prerequisite to being a godly teacher. "A little child will lead them," the Word said in Isaiah 11:6 (AMP). You can learn from anyone at any age. If we consider that the lack of godliness in our world has a direct correlation to the amount of time we spend studying God's Word, we will immediately see a need to take back the mountain of education. Not convinced? Consider this. The Word also says it is better for a millstone to be tied around your neck than to lead a little one astray (Luke 17:2). Isn't that what we are doing in education today? Are we not all stakeholders in our local school? Do we not all have a voice in the major institutions of our communities? The answer is yes, yes, and amen. We are all called to the mountain of education in one capacity or another. Each one takes a pebble, like attending a school board meeting and joining the parent-teacher organization, whether we have a child in the school or not. Or taking a boulder, like participating in community-led groups within our schools or volunteering to read to a child regularly. Some of us will be called to take a ridge on the mountain of education by running for elected office within the school government or advising curriculum teams. Some will teach. Others will write legislation. Still, others will participate in advocacy related to the educational system. But no one should be exempt from holding this mountain for the future of our society.

GOVERNMENT & LAW

Like the mountain of education, we all play a role in these cultural influences. Government and the law are lofty offices, but they are no more important than any other mountain of influence to which the Christian has been called. The United States was founded on a moral principle aligned with godliness, even though the application of those ideals was fraught with human failure. We cannot, however, be so distracted with politics that we forego our participation in taking back the mountains of government and the legal system. When I say "take back" in reference to any of these mountains, it is because we do not currently have control over them. So yes, government must be taken back for the people of God and for God's purposes. These may be a seasonal endeavor for most people. Even early politicians in republics and democracies serve terms, unlike a dictatorship or even a monarchy that has no set term for their reign.

Within the leadership of a nation, state, or community is reflected the moral condition of that community, state, or nation. Globally, we are replete with immorality. The Bible tells us to pray for those in leadership, but I dare say there is more we must do in order to use our authority as believers. Purpose, mission, and vision are communicated by the government for the people. The law enforces that purpose. On those grounds alone, we need the Spirit of God roaming the halls of our government in the persons of believing Christians. We cannot and should not expect government regulation to treat all men equally when the people in government themselves do not treat all men equally. That being said, if you are called to this area of authority, you will need prayer—lots of it. But you will be graced in your ability to carry out your authority through Christ, who strengthens you. I'll conclude with an obvious but powerful notion: Christians should be in all areas of government as elected and appointed advisors. It was thus in Jesus's day, and boy, do we need it now.

MEDIA, NEWS & COMMENTARY

As previously mentioned, there is more work to be done in the areas of media, even though we have major television networks whose purpose is to spread the gospel to all the world. The problem, as I see it, involves the misinformation that also permeates our airwaves, confusing people and causing division in communities. This is very evident in the Middle East, the United Kingdom, and America. The media, news, and commentary mountain includes sources such as TV, radio, newspapers, online news, and, of course, the hugely influential social media sites and blogs on the Internet. In some nations, we have allowed our desire for free speech to purposefully indoctrinate and propagandize our news, leaving a deadly wake of uninformed voters, activists, and social media influencers who further the corrupt messages they received.

As believers, we cannot combat the media mountain without taking an offensive position to correct and re-teach those principles Christ taught. In this message of truth, our foremost posture must be that of love. One thing Christ taught us during His ministry is that love must be the attitude through which truth is shared. Have any of you ever been corrected by the Holy Spirit? I have, and I promise you, it wasn't that bad. Meaning that even when we correct wrong thoughts, policies, or doctrines, we can do so with the love of Christ in our hearts and on our lips.

ARTS & ENTERTAINMENT

Much light has been shed on the world of arts and entertainment even before the prosecution and death of Jeffrey Epstein, a notorious sexual exploiter who offered children to many in the elite world of entertainment. Going back to a quote I recently heard from Malcolm X seems appropriate at this time. In an interview held at the University of California, Berkeley, in 1963, he said, "Comedians, musicians, and athletes are not true leaders [author's paraphrase]. Show me in the White community where a trumpet player would be considered a leader? These people [meaning specifically Black entertainers but could be applied to all entertainers today] are used as political puppets and clowns that have been set up...made celebrities...in order to control the masses."

What this speech was aimed at communicating is that we who get our marching orders, or information, from celebrities, athletes, and artists are foolish. X understood that the idolatry of celebrity would bring about misfortune not only for Blacks in America but any marginalized people in the world.

We have idolized those on the silver screen for so long that they are emboldened to share their political and other beliefs with the world as influencers. I recall a few years ago when actress Alyssa Milano came to Georgia to protest a pro-life law being voted upon in our state legislature. With her came actors and actresses dressed as midwives in hooded red capes and white aprons. These individuals stood inside our state capitol for weeks on end, harassing elected officials, all in front of media cameras from around the nation. Music, movies, television, and social media wield enormous influence on our youth, but they also build complacency and compromise into adults who spend an inordinate amount of time being entertained by the secular world. This complacency reduces our effectiveness in sharing Christ's grace in the world by allowing celebrities to stand behind the pulpit of public opinion.

BUSINESS & ECONOMICS

"Prosperity with a purpose" is a phrase I will borrow to support what I believe is a gift from God: the free market system. However, the Word of God gave many provisions for how we are to govern ourselves when it comes to business. Scriptures say that if you do not work, you don't eat (2 Thessalonians 3:10). After all, when God put Adam in the garden, He put him to work, tilling the land and tending to the animals (Genesis 2:5–7). So, there should be no question that God has called us to work and use money as a tool to preach His gospel. This burden or weight that we are responsibly urged to do is from God. The questions come in when we are challenged to leave our faith in the parking lot when we go to work. But how could we? If faith is as integral to us as it was to Jesus, then our work is the Word, and the Word is our work... This should occur whether we are wearing a uniform for the postal services or wearing a tie and sitting behind a desk. No matter what we do to gain access to the economic system, we should do it by faith, for faith purposes, and for faith people.

We've heard it said that everything is marketing. I'll add to that: everything is business. The kingdom of God is designed for us to succeed in everything we set our hands to under His providence. Who you were as a child is who you are now in that the gifts and talents He gave you were visible to heaven in your mother's womb. It is our challenge to figure out what that is. At some point in my life, I decided I wanted to be a college professor. I reached that goal in 2018, and it ended the following year. When I inquired of the Lord why I wasn't being given more courses to teach, He replied, "That was your goal that I honored, but I have other things for you to do." I was happy doing the work and was very good at it. But the fact remains: I chose to submit my business decisions in God's hands. If I made a business decision to continue to pursue a career in higher education, forsaking all other endeavors, I would be broke and miserable today. Many are the plans in a man's heart, but it is the Lord's purpose that prevails (Proverbs 19:21).

There is a business you have been called to. It may be making pies or superconductors. You may be gifted to write books but be called to government. Or perhaps you are a gifted artist but have a fear of presenting your creations to the world and instead work in a cubicle for someone else's company. The manual for our life teaches us to follow God, who is the author and finisher of our faith. In other words, the product and process we are in the business of promoting comes from Him, no matter what side hustle we prefer.

The burden or passion that God sees in us is sometimes invisible in our own eyes. But He knows why He created you, and that should be the business we focus on. Having said that, let me go against all we've been taught by the world. The propensity to do something in the kingdom of God cannot always be measured by the tests of man. It is God who calls us to a mountain of influence, and He tests us in those endeavors. Only then can we be sure we are walking in purpose and authority in business or any other field.

Let me take this discussion a bit further. Understand that according to the book of Jeremiah, before we were conceived in our mother's womb, God knew us. He created some of us as prophets, some teachers, some evangelists, some pastors, and some apostles. Perhaps you are a prophet to the government. Perhaps a teacher in media. Or an evangelist in media. Whatever and whoever you are, God created you to be that in the earth, and He desperately needs you to do your job in the authority of Christ. That's dominion and the power of purpose. It has been my experience that God cannot even trust us with the full revelation of our purpose until we (1) know our identity in Him, (2) develop disciplines that allow our giftings to come forth, and (3) walk in the freedom of understanding how providence and purpose collide to bring the promise to pass.

Perhaps you have checked all the boxes and are ready to be who God called you to be. Yet, your life does not reflect what you know in your heart to be true. This is a frustrating place to live. I know because I've lived there for years. But instead of giving up on God, the dream, or myself, I recognized the internship phase I was in. God opened the door to my purpose. He continually encourages me with words of confirmation. I feel as if I am growing in my ability to use my God-given authority in my calling. We cannot rush either the growth process or the grace process. God would not allow us to begin this journey unless we were already finished (that is, called, qualified, and equipped) to do the work. When the scripture says He knows the end from the beginning, we can rest assured that our future, which is settled in our past, is sure. Knowing your purpose and authority, which is rooted in identity, is key to petitioning the courts of heaven. It is Satan's goal to keep us from authority in purpose. More importantly, it is God's greatest goal, aside from salvation, to have us walking in purpose with authority.

Here's my final closing on the matter of authority and purpose. You are not too old to pursue purpose. It is a life-long mission. You are not too young to use your God-given authority. This is a gift given freely to the sons and daughters of God. You are not too feeble, dumb, smart, rich, poor, Black, or White to be about kingdom work. You are the one God is counting on to use the authority and power He gave you when you accepted Jesus as Lord. Purpose is more powerful than plans. Purpose is more important than plans. And purpose precedes plans. Our dreams are important to God... they are for the people of God...they are given by God. In those dreams, you have already been given the authority to walk in power.

FOUR

PETITIONING THE
MERCY COURTROOM

Now that time has been spent establishing the authority by which the mercy courtroom can be petitioned, it is important that the process about to be described is not looked at as a formula but rather a practical illustration for prayers that have been hindered, especially those hindered to the point of provoking fear. Hope deferred makes the heart sick (Proverbs 13:12). When we stand believing for a thing and are then deferred in receiving the manifestation of our desires, we can become overcome with dread and fear. We may even start to doubt God or our salvation. Most of us have been there. In fact, it may be this longing for resolution that caused some of you to pick up this book. To you, I say, Godspeed. God's speed was what I needed when He revealed to me the nature of His court system.

The revelation of heavenly courtrooms over the course of almost two decades began when the Holy Spirit recalled an encounter I had in the superior court of DeKalb County, Georgia. I had gone through a divorce, and my children's father was evading child support enforcement. Like many fathers who chose to punish their ex-wives by neglecting court-ordered support, he was jumping from job to job to avoid automatic withdrawals from his paycheck. He left a higher-paying commission job to work for minimum wage, presumably in an effort to reduce the amount of his obligation. Eventually, child support payments stopped altogether, and I was left to deal with the legal system for remedies.

Many single mothers find facing this legal challenge a daunting one, which is why enforcement services assist custodial parents in facilitating fulfillment of the court order. In my case, my ex-husband became so proficient in being one step ahead of the enforcement agencies that arrears quickly accumulated. Meanwhile, I was forced to work two jobs in order to try to make ends meet. After years of this back and forth with my ex, I finally got up the nerve to represent myself pro se in a motion for contempt of court for nonpayment of the ordered child support. I remember being so nervous about standing in front of the judge, not knowing what the proceedings were going to be like or whether or not I had a chance of even being heard.

I took a day off of work and showed up with a binder in hand that documented every payment and delinquency in my case. I also brought notes regarding other irregularities arising from our divorce, things like him being late picking up the kids from daycare, his alcohol dependency, and the living conditions my children endured over the long summer visitation. The child support was one thing. After all, I was a college dropout working two jobs trying to manage two kids in elementary school. I was drowning in debt and was hurt by the struggle I found myself in. By this time, my ex-husband owed about 23,000 dollars in back child support, which represented three years of nonpayment. I knew he didn't have that kind of money lying around, but I simply wanted someone in authority to remind him that he could not get away with shirking his financial obligation to his children.

Initially, I did not see my ex-husband seated in the courtroom on this particular day. This was not the first time I attempted to bring an action of contempt against him. Perhaps, as before, he would not show up, and the case would be bound over. Months prior to this court date, I spent weeks tracking him down in hopes of having him served a summons to appear to answer the charges of contempt. For me, that meant trying to become some kind of skip tracer who made sketchy phone calls to businesses in hopes of figuring out where he might be employed. It meant begging his family to help me navigate this crisis, and it also meant cutting corners every place I could in order to make sure my children and I had a roof over our heads. It was nightmarish, to say the least. So, when I did not see him in the courtroom, even though I knew he had been served notice to attend, I felt my heart sink as my mind continued to race. Moments before the calendar was called, a person from the family law center tapped me on the shoulder. He was there to mediate a settlement between my former spouse and me on the issue of arrears. I reluctantly followed this man out of the courtroom into an adjoining room furnished with two chairs and a table. My ex-husband was seated there waiting.

When our eyes met, I immediately knew mediation was not a realistic option. What was owed was what was owed. I had triple-checked the math, which was also calculated by the Department of Children and Family Services. I had no intention of being manhandled out of my original court order. However, the mediator told me that an attempt to mediate the amount would be expected by the judge and was simply part of the process. Our divorce decree stipulated he paid the minimum amount (about 20 percent of his income) established by the state base on his salary at the time, which amounted to a 650-dollar-a-month payment for two children. This was barely enough to cover two weeks of childcare. His job change would have necessitated a modification in the value of the order, but at the time of this hearing, my ex was working in a bar for tips and had no verifiable income that could be considered by the courts at all.

The Georgia Child Support Recovery Act was amended in 2003 to account for income-shared determination rather than mere percentage-based determination. The amendment also includes a thirty-six-month evaluation to help child support enforcement keep up with the changes in a divorce or alimony case. My case was being considered in the late 1990s, when there were no such provisions. It was just me and my ex in a room arguing over whether or not the court order was fair. At the end of the mediation, we settled the arrears on a two-to-one evaluation and prepared to stand in front of the judge. After hearing the evidence, the judge found the defendant to be in contempt of court. Two orders resulted from that judgment. First, my ex was ordered to begin paying child support in accordance with the original divorce decree at 650 dollars a month. He was further ordered to pay an additional 50 dollars per month toward the mediated arrears. I knew as well as anyone that if my ex would not pay the original amount, I could hold my breath on the arrears until I turned blue in the face. Honestly, I was fine with that. I just wanted to be able to count on the child support being consistently paid from the original order.

"What if," I asked the judge, "he does not follow your order?" The judge responded, "Then bring him back, and we will arrest him for contempt." As the gavel dropped, so did my ex-husband's head. Part of me wondered, "Why not arrest him now?" He was already found in contempt. Getting to this judgment was strenuous. I couldn't imagine having to go through it again.

Although none of this was funny, it was comical to see how fervently my children's father tried to convince everyone in that courtroom that he would have no problem whatsoever paying this new child support order. Thirty days came and went, and no payment was made.

I immediately went back to court. The case was presented before the same judge, naturally. As I stood there, representing myself with no shoulder to even cry on, I reminded the judge what he said about being in contempt. My ex did not show up to this hearing—not only was he not formerly served, but he also likely feared being arrested if he had shown up. Again, I stood before the bench, my notebook in hand. I showed the bailiff the previous decision of the court and asked for a legal remedy. To that request, the judge asked me the most peculiar question. He asked, "Where is your ex-husband?"

I looked around the courtroom again.

"He is not here."

"I cannot do anything if he is not present," the judge responded. "Why isn't he here?"

"Sir, it took me months to track him down to get him here before. I spent the last little bit of money I had paying for a process server. I don't even know where he is." All of this was true. I couldn't believe I was expected to get my ex to court. If his kids were not enough to get him to pay child support, what impact could my pleas make? I felt a bit like Cain asking God if I was his keeper.

The judge looked at me, holding the previous contempt order in his hand, and said, "This is not a self-executing judgment. You have to get him back in court if you want something to happen." Again, the gavel fell as this petition for contempt was thrown out. I left that courtroom despondent and defeated. I had done everything I knew to do in my physical and legal power. Every remedy I sought was not enough to make sure my children received what they were legally entitled to. It was as if the previous two judgments were insufficient to secure the legal remedy they were intended to provide. That was the last time I took my ex to court for back child support. Some twelve years later, when my eldest turned eighteen, I closed my case in the online portal with the Child Support Enforcement Agency within DFACS (Department of Children and Family Services). One of their agents reopened the case, assuming it was closed in error. When I reclosed the case again, the agency demanded both my ex-husband and me return to the superior court. We were summoned to do so.

I had no intent of missing another day of work for the pleasure of being in the DeKalb County Courthouse. From my point of view, this was a closed case, but it was not my point of view that determined the proceedings. The DFCAS representative met us outside the courtroom prior to the calendar being called. By that time, my ex had accumulated over 40 thousand dollars in back child support, monies I gave up hoping and wishing for. After all, my daughter was eighteen and headed off to college. My son was well into high school and thriving. Somehow, some way, I had made ends meet enough to get these kids through, even without the help of their father. Holding a grudge against him for the years of struggle and hard times did nothing for me. After coming to a more complete faith, I learned the power of forgiveness to give freedom to the captive. When I explained to the representative that I was captive to this debt, as was my children's father, she shook her head in disbelief. But forgiving the debt released us both and closed my case with the enforcement agency for good.

Years later, I found myself deep in prayer about a concern that was pressing on my heart. It was about a delay I was experiencing for which I could not account. I asked God to search my heart to find the source of the delay. After doing so, I prayed fervently for God to fulfill His promise to me. When the prayer was concluded, and the "amens" said, I heard the Holy Spirit tell me that I had just prayed a self-executing order. Immediately, I was reminded of the child support case from years prior. That superior court judge explained that a self-executing order would have automatically caused a series of events to take place from the moment my ex-husband missed the first payment of the new order. He was to be picked up by the police if he fell into arrears again. Every consequence of his actions was to be put into motion without any effort on my part. In fact, what the judge was saying was that my part was done. The rest, he informed, would have been the responsibility of the court. However, unlike in the words spoken to my spirit in prayer, the judge in my child support case never signed the contempt order as a self-executing one. But as God reminded me of those proceedings, I began to understand how God's courtroom works.

Was I praying according to His will? Yes. Did I pray in belief, lacking doubt and double-mindedness? Yes. Was I praying in the season appropriated for recompense? Yes. Have I seen the manifestation of this prayer? Not completely, although, like a large steamer, things have begun turning in my favor. The truth is, I have stayed in perfect peace about this request from that moment until this moment because of the self-executing order in my favor. At the time this occurred, I hadn't thought about the mercy courtroom as an actual place. I was taught to petition the throne of grace with prayers and thanksgiving, something I did routinely. Certainly, a throne room and a courtroom conjure different mental pictures in our minds. At the time, I did not understand that mercy and grace are synonymous, nor did I realize that God's throne is a type of judgment seat. What am I saying? When we petition the throne of grace, we, in fact, petition the mercy courtroom.

Let's be super clear. Courtrooms here on earth and courtrooms in heaven all have protocols they follow. When we are unaware of or ill-prepared to follow those protocols, we risk delaying a judgment of favor. Like me, when I pleaded my own case with the court to execute its own order of contempt, I was without an intermediary who understood the legal grounds for my petition. The legal representation that would have been useful in my case against my former spouse is fulfilled in the person of Jesus Christ when we petition the courts of heaven. In fact, no matter which courtroom we seek a legal remedy in, Jesus and His blood act not only as an advisory counselor but as petitioner, solicitor general, legal eagle, and main mouthpiece in petitioning God's hand when a perceived delay causes fear, doubt, and faintness of heart. Matthew 24 talks about the elect, God's set-apart ones, falling away or losing heart. This is God's desire: that we all serve in a kind of fullness that does not lose heart.

Trust me. I understand the desire to give up. I understand growing weary in well-doing. But I believe God has revealed not only a way to accelerate mercy but also secure steadfastness in the waiting. My child support woes were where God began to teach me about His mercy courtroom. He continued those lessons as I fought a medical diagnosis.

By my late thirties, I had undergone several surgeries for endometriosis. The treatments and pain I endured in between broke me as a woman. I truly had no will to fight for my health. I'd seen traditional doctors as well as holistic ones. Nothing seemed to make a difference, and I didn't know how many more surgeries I could endure. I desperately wanted another child, but a hysterectomy was becoming inevitable. I remember crawling on the floor of my master bathroom, weakened by blood loss and debilitated by fear. I was alone in this struggle and embarrassed by my condition. Through tears, I asked God to help—that's all I could manage to utter. A month or so later, I had another surgery.

When I opened my eyes from the surgery, my doctor was staring at me just a few inches from my face.

"Am I dead?" It seemed like a reasonable enough question.

"No," he followed with a smile that broke the starkness of his previous stare.

Then he proceeded to tell me that my bowels and womb had been tangled in the endometrial tissue overgrowth, which twisted them into knots. He said when he cut my womb loose, it jumped about three inches above my abdomen and then went back to its original place. He had never witnessed a reaction like that before. While I appreciated the medical uniqueness of my case, I just wanted to feel normal. As it was, this was my sixth abdominal surgery, and I was tired. After that surgery, I was diagnosed with endometrial cancer and had a full hysterectomy. The recovery and hormone therapy were painful. Depression set in. My second husband left me in this process of healing, and I gave up on life. But God was faithful to that bathroom prayer.

Sixteen months after my hysterectomy, I stopped the hormone replacement therapies. Supernaturally, my estrogen levels were normal. Hot flashes ended abruptly. My mood recovered. Even though I was getting divorced, for the first time in my life, I didn't have abdominal pain. I was healed. Fifteen years later, I found myself facing not one but two cancer possibilities.

I'm not sure cancer survivors ever forget the pain of past experiences. I was taken right back to my hysterectomy when my current doctors told me that they found a growth in my lungs and kidneys. While I was visibly rocked by the diagnosis, I was also strong in my knowledge of God's healing power, and I was determined to fight even more than I had fought before. Initially, what I meant by fighting was quite different than what it turned out to be.

When I had endometrial cancer, I cried all the time. I was physically weak and despondent. It was a painful and lengthy process that eventually led to healing. I didn't want to go through that again. Somehow, I held on to the truth of God's power to heal, but I didn't want it to be a process that spanned years. I couldn't handle that again, and I knew death was premature if it came at this time. I had no choice but to petition the throne room.

For a few weeks, I studied everything I could find on the throne room. I prayed in my native tongue and heavenly language. I began taking Communion and did all the things I knew to do in the natural, including taking a high blood pressure medication. At night, I stayed up and prayed until I fell asleep. I tried to watch my words and only speak healing. I had healing verses on sticky notes and really tried to hold it together. But after a month of scans, hearing that the mass on my lungs was nine centimeters long and the mass on my liver was 3.5 centimeters turned me into a babbling mess. I couldn't even make it through an MRI without crying.

I was lying in bed watching Netflix when I remembered what someone from my Bible study had said earlier that day. "Why can we spend hours completing a series on Netflix," they said, "but we struggle to give God the same amount of time in prayer?" They continued, "Instead of spending time with God, many of us will just chill out with Netflix and let the enemy get a stronghold." The Holy Spirit brought those words to life in me as I scrolled the movie titles on the app. I had to decide whether to yield to tiredness and frustration or preserve in faith. I chose the latter.

Immediately, I turned the lights on and the television off. I got on my hands and knees and began to pray. In my mind's eye, I pictured myself approaching God's mercy courtroom, and there I began to petition. Some may choose to pray beforehand about their entrance into the courts of heaven. There is nothing inherently wrong with submitting yourself to God and asking for godly counsel even to approach the courtroom. I had a prophetic dream about this some years ago. In the dream, I was dressed in a wedding gown and headed to the sanctuary from which I was to be married. As I moved through the outer rooms of the church, I realized I did not have shoes on. Sensing the time was nearing for the ceremony to start, I debated whether or not I should return to my hotel room for shoes or simply walk down the aisle barefooted. Guests who were dressed in their Sunday best were making their way to the sanctuary but did not appear to be concerned that I, the perceived bride, was ill-prepared to walk down the aisle. Chapel bells began to ring as if calling all those invited to the marriage supper of the Lamb to take their places in the sanctuary. In the dream, I made the decision to run back to my hotel room and grab my shoes; however, seeing as time was of the essence, I held them in my hand so I could run back to the chapel in time for the wedding ceremony.

As I entered the church, I noticed people seated outside the inner sanctuary enjoying beverages and snacks. They were engaged in supposed godly conversation. But they had no strong desire to enter into the ceremony to take part. "How," I wondered, "could they be satisfied with being outside of this inner circle who were about to witness the marriage of the Lamb?" As I opened the double doors to the sanctuary, I realized I was but one of many in the bridal party making our way to the bema or altar. As we approached our High Priest, I realized through the Holy Spirit that some would be satisfied with being invited to the wedding as guests rather than participating as the bride.

I believe the courts of heaven are similar in that it is by faith that we will have intimate access to the things of God. As we realize that the spiritual part of us is just as meaningful as our flesh, even more so, we can gain a better perspective of what it means to live by faith. To step into a heavenly dimension, we only need to recognize that our worthiness is through the blood of the Lamb. Furthermore, we submit ourselves to the power of the Lamb as we accept that He has granted us access to approach as the bride, not merely a guest. In other words, we have a right through Jesus's righteousness to operate in the rulership of heaven, which is higher than those things of earth. Finally, we understand, not just in mind but in heart as well, that the unrighteousness branded upon us does not have to be the final word or work, for that matter. Those ill-gotten judgments are the antithesis of God's divine design for our lives and, therefore, can come under the jurisdiction of the blood covenant granted us through a belief in Jesus Christ. Legally, Jesus made a way.

Understand this: I cannot tell you what the courtroom should look like or explain its ecological characteristics because, frankly, that is not important. Just as with any prayer, it is the spirit behind the petitions that makes the difference. For me, the fighting spirit was upon me, and I knew it. It gave me a boldness, like Acts 4:24, and I understood I was speaking in authority given to me by Jesus's blood. There is a moment in faith when the anointing from heaven falls. Some experience this corporately in church, others do so in their own quiet times. My experience has been that when the anointing falls, there is an open door to heaven. I have since come to know that our availability to petition God's courtroom has no limits. It is always open to us. But in the beginning of petitioning the mercy courtroom, I moved when I was moved by the anointing of God's Spirit.

Years of being under good teaching reminded me that our prayers, our enemy, and the elders are before the throne (Revelation 4; Job 1). Aside from Genesis and Esther, Revelation was one of the only books of the Bible I read as a young person. I knew it better than any other (which is all relative). The point I am making is that there was a scriptural basis for what I was seeing in my mind's eye as I prayed. I saw myself, much like a natural courtroom, approaching the throne to petition on my behalf.

I knew God could heal; I had seen it in my own life. But speeding up healing, which is what I was asking for, I had no basis for. All I could stand on was the fact that:

- When we pray, heaven hears (1 John 5:15; 2 Chronicles 7:14).

- There are witnesses in heaven who testify on our behalf (Hebrews 12:1).

- Jesus is my intermediary (Romans 8:34; Hebrews 7:24–25).

- The blood of Jesus speaks a better way (Hebrews 12:24).

- There is a promised inheritance guaranteed by the Spirit of God to His select (Ephesians 1:14).

Each one of these truths had been previously revealed to me by the Holy Spirit and brought to my attention in this moment of prayer. I began to petition for God's mercy to be appropriated on my behalf. With eyes tightly shut and still on all fours, I grew in spiritual stamina and belief. Now remember, prostrating oneself, crying, lighting candles, or any other rituals are not prerequisites for God to act on our behalf. We are spirits and should be, therefore, led by the Spirit. I was groaning, and that's why I was on all fours. I truly believe that our prayer posture is individual and should be a natural position based on our relationship with Jesus. The words I prayed, however, can be personalized and used by any believer.

With personalized prayers, for example, taking a scripture and inserting your own name in the place of the Bible character, is a type of spiritual practice that can yield strength, encouragement, and a reward. I do not believe it was God's intent to confirm every word to our spirit separately from His written Word. What I mean by that is, if you find a scriptural basis to pray on, go for it. Generally speaking, you do not need confirmation to do so; however, the Holy Spirit does have a way of confirming words to us through nature, a neighbor, circumstances, and other teaching. However, this is, in my experience, far different than praying based on a Rhema Word from God. For example, if a word from God goes off in your spirit and is illuminated to your mind, it is a word given in a specific season or time. Meaning, right now is the time to pray regarding that concern. When petitioning the mercy courtroom, I find you can be most effective when you have both a Rhema Word, utterance or groaning, and a general word from the scripture. In other words, when a combination of both spiritual senses and natural senses collide in a moment in time.

When I began to address or call on those who would be present in the courtroom, I heard the Lord speak a Rhema Word to me. It is like when Jesus healed the lepers who received their healing as they took a step in faith (Luke 17:11). Just for clarification's sake, when I say "call" on those to be present in the courtroom, I am not talking about conjuring spirits. There is an evil counterfeit that occurs in occult practices that manipulate the spirit realm, such as tarot card and palm reading, crystal divination, potions, herbs, incantations, necromancy, and other pagan rituals that are in opposition to God's ways. These things lead only to death. However, petitioning the mercy courtroom calls on your (as the petitioner) knowledge or understanding of the parties that are already in front of the court.

The Bible gives us the precedent from which to follow. First, we understand that God is seated on His throne. If we petition His mercy, we do so under the authority through which mercy is dispensed. For years, I knew God as Savior but never knew Him as Father. It took years, decades, for me to see God as my Father because I did not have an earthly example that resembled God's fatherhood, and I struggled to understand God the Father. In other words, it would be manipulative of me if I chose to pray to the Father out of obligation or ritual because I did not know Him as Father. It is the same way with the mercy courtroom. If you do not personally know of God's mercy, you have no business in the mercy courtroom. However, I believe, and it stands to reason, that you do not have to be present to have a judgment in your own favor in the mercy courtroom. The blood of Jesus and the Holy Spirit, our legal counsel, can petition the Just Judge on our behalf even without our presence.

Second, we have to believe that the great cloud of witnesses can witness on our behalf. Hebrews 12:1 teaches us that the prayers of those who have gone before us act as witnesses. We are equipped to throw off every sin and entangling hindrance because God has set us up for success. I cannot teach you how to believe in these things. Scriptures say we must work out our own salvation with fear and trembling (Philippians 2:12). But I can tell you that if you ask for something in God's will, He will provide all good gifts to His children. When I first got saved, I pursued God with fervor. By knowing God and seeking Him first, I began to know the things of God. Once in prayer, I was graced by a visitation of the cloud of witnesses in my backyard. From that moment forward, no one can ever convince me that Hebrews 12 *isn't* true. I imagine them seated like a jury might be in a courtroom. How foolish it would be to walk into a courtroom and not acknowledge those who witness what is going on and have the right to testify. The same can be said for the mercy courtroom. The cloud of witnesses will be there whether you recognize them or not.

The third thing I address complements the second. I ask for the books of remembrance to be opened and read on my behalf. I have come to believe that the witnesses offer testimony based on what is recorded in the books of remembrance. Much like the story of Mordecai in the book of Esther, God's kingdom has a mirror image here on earth. When King Artaxerxes read that nothing had been done to reward Mordecai the Jew for his heroic deed, it was immediately rectified because there was a witness or written record. I further believe that the prayers of the righteous avail much, according to James 5:16. Depending on my petition, in this case, healing, I know that prayers of my family members before me have been for the benefit of my bloodline. So, I appropriate those prayers in my favor and present them as part of my case. Just because my loved ones have translated to another life, it does not invalidate the prayers spoken in faith.

While I am not sure there is any law regarding the order in which these statements have been made in faith, I have simply acknowledged what I saw in my mind's eye, knowing that Jesus is on the right hand of the Father. As I identify how I address the mercy courtroom in this book, I do so based on what I see, left to right.

Once the bench (or throne), witnesses, and books of remembrance have been acknowledged, I ask for my adversary to be present and silent. This I learned from God's Foundation Builders Ministries (GFBI) in Moravian Falls, North Carolina. GFBI has many videos on accessing the courts of heaven when there are occult or generational curses operating in a believer's bloodline. In those instances, especially, I can see why having the prosecution's star witness (Satan) present is important. The most exciting part of this entire prayer is the request that he be present but silent.

From there, I ask for the blood of Jesus to speak on my behalf. This is the most crucial protocol in petitioning the mercy courtroom. Jesus's blood and our relationship with Him are what grant us access to the courts of heaven. Without His blood speaking for us, we have no case. Furthermore, I separately ask Jesus to be present as an advocate. In other words, Jesus is like our attorney, and God's Holy Spirit our mediator. Since it has been said that Father God sees us, or judges us, through the blood, it must be liberally applied or represented in court so that our petitions receive their due. Just as in a man-made courtroom, it is wise to present every shred of evidence while in front of the bench. Any protocol we fail to utilize for our benefit is like showing up to court without having taken steps to advance a favorable outcome.

Have you started making a mental picture yet? You stand before the mercy courtroom's bench with Father God at the helm. You have acknowledged the cloud of witnesses and the books of remembrance (your personal book according to Malachi 3:16, KJV, and the books of those bound to you by covenant). You have summoned your enemy to be present and silent. Jesus and His blood are present on your behalf. It is time for you to present your case. When I first did this, it was the physical healing of cancer. Specifically, I asked for the nodule on my lung to shrink and the abnormal cell mass in my kidney to dissolve. Don't ask me why I didn't just pray for both masses to dissolve, but in the moment, I kept replaying what my doctor reported. He was threatening me to take me into surgery.

In my mind, nine centimeters stuck out to me. I wanted it to be smaller—the size was a factor. So, I prayed that it would shrink. The size of the mass relative to the size of my kidney was so large that I prayed for it to dissolve. Again, size was a factor, but, in this case, the tumor measured large compared to the size of my kidney. With each organ, I made my petitions known. As I prayed, I heard the Holy Spirit, our mediator, speak to my heart. He impressed me to understand that traditional medicine was not the children's bread. The Gospel of Matthew Chapter Fifteen describes an encounter Jesus had with a Canaanite woman in the region of Tyre. This woman had a demon-possessed daughter and sought Jesus for her child's healing.

Throughout Jesus's ministry, He had been harassed by the Pharisees and scribes. This day was no different. After warding off an inquisition about His disciples and their practices, Jesus withdrew from the crowds only to encounter this desperate mother. The text reads:

> "Have mercy on me, Lord, you son of David! My daughter is severely possessed by a demon!"

> But he answered her not a word. His disciples came and begged him, saying, "Send her away; for she cries after us."

But he answered, "I wasn't sent to anyone but the lost sheep of the house of Israel."

But she came and worshiped him, saying, "Lord, help me."

But he answered, "It is not appropriate to take the children's bread and throw it to the dogs."

But she said, "Yes, Lord, but even the dogs eat the crumbs which fall from their masters' table."

Then Jesus answered her, "O woman, great is your faith! Let it be to you as you desire." And her daughter was healed from that very hour.

Matthew 15:22–28 (NKJV)

Traditional medicine is not the children's bread. What I understood the Holy Spirit to say to me was that I could receive healing through doctors and prescribed treatments, or I could receive a supernatural impartation that resulted in healing like this woman's child. I knew I did not want to endure a lengthy process as I had with the cancer before. I also had grown in faith over those fifteen years and had received healing for a brain tumor. I felt confident in this Rhema Word that God was opening the windows of heaven for me to ask for complete healing at that moment. So, I approached the mercy seat in boldness, reminding Him of the prayers I personally prayed on behalf of my bloodline. I reminded God of the words of knowledge that had been spoken over me but were not yet fulfilled. I prayed God's Word in the courtroom, recalling those scriptures that were engraved on my heart. In short, I spoke in faith and in power.

To seal all that had been spoken, I appropriated my knowledge of the legal system in this heavenly place.

I asked that this judgment be in my favor as a final decree recorded in the books of remembrance.

I asked that the order be self-executing.

I asked that the judgment be to a thousand generations in my bloodline. In other words, I bound cancer from my descendants as a result of these proceedings.

I asked that the blood speak on my behalf when it came to matters of my health and that it, the blood, have the final authority.

I repented for ways I had mistreated my temple (body) or spoken against God's Word concerning my health.

I took my rightful authority over cancer, restraining or binding it by order of the blood and this mercy courtroom.

I asked for any future action in this matter to be denied, noting that the enemy had no legal authority over my health.

I presented these prayers and petitions to the Just Judge, addressing the Father as such, in this courtroom, and thanked Him for a judgment in my favor.

To that end, I praised God for a little while and fell asleep. A few weeks later, I was at the respiratory doctor's office, preparing to hear either the good news or a mandate to go directly into surgery. My expectation was for healing. But as I sat there listening to the doctor's report, not once but twice, I was overcome with laughter. I was filled with joy and peace that passed all understanding because all I could dwell on was the fact that Satan heard the judgment in my favor and had to keep his mouth shut. He could not accuse me because I repented and then presented overwhelming evidence by grace through faith in the blood of Jesus Christ. As my doctor began to tell me that the tumor had shrunk down to eleven millimeters (basically the size of an English pea) down from nine centimeters (small grapefruit size), I lost all concern for the mass in my kidneys. That appointment was another two weeks away in a different doctor's office. As with many medically trained professionals, our reaction to miraculous news can sometimes make them question our sanity rather than recognize the miracle. It matters not. God healed my lungs, and I went into the urologist's office expecting the best.

From the time I was twenty-three, I've had health challenges, most of which I treated through traditional medicine. There was a time when I used homeopathic remedies combined with prayer to alleviate symptoms and more. From now on, I will only petition the Just Judge in His mercy courtroom because I understand that healing is, in fact, the children's bread. The urologist reported that the mass on my kidney must have been a phantom because there was nothing there on the follow-up scans. It was gone.

WHY THE MERCY COURTROOM?

The enemy comes to steal, kill, and destroy (John 10:10). For example, public ignorance about environmental cancers has hurt and even killed many. Companies that intentionally deceived consumers and kept them ignorant about the threats acted as agents of evil. They were used by our enemy to destroy life. Another example of the enemy using an involuntary or inherited disease to kill or destroy, such as heart arrhythmias, Crohn's disease, multiple sclerosis, and things of that nature, which can easily be classified as ways the enemy has come in from some legal precedent to steal purpose, kill the body, and destroy families. When those precedents exist, petitioning God's mercy is well within His will and plan for us. These are perfect "cases" for the mercy courtroom from my point of view. This is not to say that other things do not warrant mercy, but it must be our primary interest to seek God regarding the application of mercy rather than other judgments that are available to us through the blood of Jesus Christ and our relationship with Him. Many of us understand that through ignorance, we have become victims of our enemy's legal right to torment us. Perhaps that has not been your experience. Consider the shared history of humanity through a prophetic lens. In Genesis, the curse fell on all mankind, the descendants of Adam, because the change in legal authority from mankind to earth's fallen state occurred as a result of sin. This, believers understand. However, we also understand that Jesus has become our advocate to the Father, representing us, because of the remission of sin secured in His blood. His purpose was to reclaim authority over earth and present it back to us, re-establishing God's kingdom on earth. Jesus was appointed by God to do these things. If these two truths are settled in your mind, then consider that it is ignorance about the judgment in our favor through Christ that allows the enemy to continue to use legalism against us. Christ's appointment in the mercy courtroom establishes the righteousness through which earthly changes are eligible. That eligibility is the authority, but that authority must be appropriated in our lives. That is where mercy can come in.

God's Word states that we will reap in due season if we faint not (Galatians 6:9). This scripture was written by Paul to the church in Galatia; however, it can be activated on our behalf.

FIVE

PETITIONS, PROCEEDINGS, AND THE JUDGMENT SEAT

When we operate in earthly courtrooms, we do so under the authority of a government. We do so whether or not we understand the ways in which the courts work and whether or not we voted for the government in power. We are mere subjects to the proceedings set before us. In this mindset, let us look at the kingdom of God through which we have our citizenship. We read in Matthew 28:18 that all authority in heaven and earth was given to Jesus. He is the head of the kingdom. Who gave Him that power? God, His Father. Since we know Jesus is in God, as He is God, and God the Father is in Him, we can picture a joint rulership in the kingdom of heaven. When God said in the beginning, "Let us make man in our own image," He described Himself as a Triune God, as His Spirit was the first to act as an agent of the kingdom here on earth. It is these proceedings we must learn to understand.

We read in John 6 that no one can come to the Father unless the Father gives us the desire to come (to Jesus). If we have been given that desire and accepted Jesus, we are well positioned to petition the judgment seat of heaven. We have to let the Lord work out our ability to come into the legal system of heaven, which supersedes the laws of the countries in which we currently live. Because of this divine authority, we can petition heaven for what we need to accomplish the things God has called us to do on earth. Let's agree that it is in God's best interest to honor the gifting of authority He put in us because His character and reputation are tied to His image-bearers, us. As mature Christians, we have a role to play in learning about the way God runs His government.

As image-bearers who are called by God's name, we fall under the jurisdiction of the kingdom of heaven. We operate, or we are intended to operate, with full access to the warehouses of heaven, from which we can requisition through petition that which we need. Additionally, we can be judged according to the purposes God called us to fulfill. This is all good news. Although, most of us have not considered what we have access to as children of God.

Now that we have established the origin of our authority and settled the citizenship question, we have to conclude that for which we can petition. In my view, petitions to the mercy seat are different from petitions to the judgment seat. This chapter will attempt to differentiate the two courtrooms that we have access to.

What we call a "Hail Mary" in American football is a last-ditch effort set on a wing and a prayer in hopes of reaching the endzone and giving the team something to cheer about. That's a mercy-type prayer. There is a difference between a Hail Mary that is honored by God out of His goodness and a requisition of heaven prayer that someone operating in God's authority petitions heaven for. While angels may play a role in everything that comes out of heaven, I consider authoritative prayers as directed toward angels through God's throne because Hebrews 1:14 reminds us that there are angels meant to serve those who inherit salvation. That's us!

Let's look at a practical example. When a person working for a company needs a file from the file room, they follow the processes and procedures in place to requisition the file. If they need a replacement ink cartridge for the printer, they requisition it and the company pays for it. Whatever they need to do the job, it is the company's responsibility to make it happen. God's kingdom is no different. In fact, God's kingdom invented this kind of efficiency. The only caveat, if you will, is that the requisition must be approved by someone in authority. Again, that's us! That is part of the justification process. When you hear "judgment seat," imagine justification.

When God told me to start a school, I was a classroom teacher with moderate experience. Like David, I was in the field with the sheep. No one would have said I was headmaster material yet.

However, God justified me when He called me to do this work. He gave me the authority to requisition heaven for the materials I would need to carry out the call. God calls. God justifies, God equips. He finances the call. In this way, God creates the path or opportunity for us to walk in the fullness of our purpose.

As I researched the process of becoming a headmaster, I discovered that I needed to earn a Ph.D. to hold the title in an accredited school. Notice that I did not go out and start telling parents to send me their kids because I had a school. God does all things in decency and order. Oftentimes, His order is unknown to us, so we must study to show ourselves that we are approved. When I decided to go back to school to pursue this advanced degree, I didn't see myself doing homework again. I didn't see myself paying out of pocket for classes. Frankly, I didn't see myself as a headmaster. But I knew I heard from God. The Word had been confirmed, and there was a process that led to the calling.

It's actually an interesting story. I had taken a job in an area of town I thought I knew about. I had worked just five miles down the road for years. I understood the community and the students I would be serving. To my surprise, this new assignment was nothing like I expected. The student body was made up predominantly of refugees. These were kids who had seen the worse of humanity and were now in a foreign country, sitting in front of me. The staff and administration team at this large elementary school were very strict. They had high expectations for all students, whether they could speak English or not. I was intimidated and in over my head. But the very first week of school, I heard the Lord tell me to learn how to open a school from Ms. Malone, the principal. *Okay*, I thought, as I fixed my face when they told me how many students would be in my classroom.

How I prayed could I teach this many students from this many cultures with this much "baggage." It would take a miracle, and that's what I prayed for. I began petitioning the judgment seat of God for the grace to do this job. I learned that it would take more than grace to reach these kids—I needed strategies as well. I needed more patience than I had. I needed a will not to quit. I needed a supernatural flow of energy to be mentored by the principal while teaching in deep water. These were things I had access to in the inventories of heaven.

There are five scripture references about the windows of heaven that make for a great Word study when it comes to petitioning the judgment seat. For us, it makes perfect sense to start from the beginning in Genesis 7:11 with the flood. Noah, of course, was a man who found favor in the sight of the Lord as being righteous. This is a key for you and me, who need resources from heaven. First, God must find us righteous or "in the authority" to requisition resources. You might pause and say to yourself, "The flood was not about resources; it was about destruction and judgment." To that, I reply, "Not for Noah."

The ark was fifty feet tall, 450–510 feet long, and about seventy-five feet wide. Since there had been no rain on the earth, tell me, "Where were the forests from which Noah and his sons got the gopher wood?" Most historians believe gopher wood was a mistranslation from *kopher wood*, which means pitched wood in Hebrew. Some say it was cypress or cedar wood, regardless of what kind of forests they would have found in that place between the rivers. Genesis 5:28–31 records Lamech's hopes about the life his son Noah might live. Noah was born at a time when the land was dry and life was hard. Besides getting the wood, what shipbuilding school did Noah attend? Did his sons also attend or simply read Noah's crib notes at night? Of course, I am making light of the fact that Noah himself was not equipped in the natural to be obedient to God's directive, but he made a decision to be obedient to his heart. This put Noah in a position to petition the judgment seat for downloads from heaven for wood, desk plans, endurance, and everything in between to build this ark. He likely petitioned for the right words and favor to convince his sons to join him in this great building project. Recall he endured a hundred years of mockery at the hands of his neighbors as he built the ark. Tell me that it was not a supernatural grace on him that allowed him to contend with his circumstances.

How many of Noah's neighbors stopped inviting him to dinner? If they did, it was simply to belittle him. He became an outcast in the community and was on the receiving end of all jokes. The local idiot. But he staggered not at the calling on him and his family. When we open our minds to the story behind the story of Noah, we understand that God enabled him to build the ark and be a special part of God's great narrative. Listen, I am not saying wood fell from heaven outside Noah's home, but manna fell three feet thick for forty years when God needed it to. I am also not saying that the animals who boarded the ark were docile and eagerly awaiting their first cruise, but it is pretty obvious that this is exactly what happened. God judged Noah as righteous; therefore, whatever he needed to complete this task was available to him who believed.

There is no scripture reference to tell us that Noah talked to God daily, but there is a scripture that indicates God spoke and Noah heard. Folks, we can petition in our hearts, and God still hears. So, when we read that the windows of heaven and the floodgates opened up in Genesis 7, we might do well to consider that the provision of heaven, not only to build the ark but to survive the trip, poured out as well. Remember, God sees the end from the beginning. He plans in that way as well. No matter how God chose to provide for Noah physically, emotionally, and spiritually when enduring the building project and subsequent flood, we know He did.

The second scripture referenced concerning the windows of heaven is found in Isaiah 24. This, too, is a story of judgment in which the prophet saw current and future tragedies for mankind. Isaiah offers the people a preview of what is to come when the Lord's judgment is poured out. Certainly, the fire and brimstone we've all heard preached are not the only things coming out of heaven. Surely goodness and mercy, says Psalm 23, will follow us all the days of our lives.

SIX
THE COURT OF APPEALS

It is not unusual for us to question appealing a decision we have made to heaven for redemption or restoration. After all, most of us have been conditioned to believe that what goes around, comes around, and for that matter, the Bible teaches that you reap what you sow (Galatians 6:7). In the Eastern part of the world, the word "karma" might be inserted into this conversation. In the Western world, words like "fate" and "serendipity" might come into play. If you are reading this book, your nation has likely been touched by the British Crown historically. Great Britain, over the course of time, colonized most of the developing world today. While many nations resented the forced appropriation of British culture on their society, they might still credit the period of colonization for opening economic doors and creating societal structures that led to twenty-first-century invention and commerce. However, we also understand that owing allegiance to a crown gives men little authority on the earth. In fact, it was American philosopher John Locke who penned words to summarize the state of those in the Commonwealth nations under the rule of King Georgia III, saying,

> And where the body of the people, or any single man, is deprived of their right, or is under the exercise of a power without right, and have no appeal on earth, then they have a liberty to appeal to heaven, whenever they judge the cause of sufficient moment. And therefore, though the people cannot be judge, so as to have, by the constitution of that society, any superior power, to determine and give effective sentence in the case; yet they have, by a law antecedent and paramount to all positive laws of men, reserved that ultimate determination to themselves which belongs to all mankind, where there lies no appeal

on earth, viz. to judge, whether they have just cause to make their appeal to heaven.

The "appeal to heaven" flag, which flew over maritime installments in the Massachusetts colony, was supported by five nations in the Haudenosaunee (Iroquois) Confederacy, including the Seneca, Cayuga, Onondaga, Oneida, and Mohawk nations. Skennenrahawi, called the Great Peacemaker, was the leader of Haudenosaunee during a time predating the Boston Tea Party when the flag bearing New England's eastern white pine tree on a white field was flown in the northern colonies refuting the divine right of kings. Designed by Colonel Joseph Reed after being inspired by the Haudenosaunee peace, the flag was established in the Massachusetts General Court in 1776 for the five ships General Washington commissioned. The Pine Tree Riot was actually the first act of independence American colonists made, with the blessing of their First Nation neighbors. It became a symbol of resistance, and at least one signer of the Declaration of Independence credited Locke's words for inspiring the Declaration from the quote referenced in this chapter, taken from *Two Treatises of Government*. Penned in the Founding Era, *Two Treatises* was the most quoted work from 1760–1776. Yet prior to Britain's colonial reign, appeals to heaven ensued during the Babylonian, Assyrian, and Egyptian captivities. These appeals represent more than one man's cry but the cry of an entire community. Second Corinthians 5 speaks to the appeals God makes through us. This is the chapter that teaches us we are a new creation in Christ. It also reminds us that as grafted sons and daughters in the ministry of reconciliation, we act as ambassadors on earth to that which is of heaven. In other words, we are the ones who communicate heavenly ways as Christ's representatives. The appeals to the lost come through us. Upon traveling to Ephesus with Pricilla and Aquila, the apostle Paul uses the word "appeal" in his direct petitions to the church that we be in unity, living as children of light because we are those ambassadors whom the Holy Spirit partners with in the world today.

This understanding of our duty as believers overcomes Job's complaint in Chapter Nine when he says there is no arbitrator between God and man. Job's opponent in dialogue was God Himself. Jesus solved that dilemma, as does the Holy Spirit, interceding on our behalf. Frankly, it is God's Holy Spirit who teaches us lovingly where we have erred. I use the word "where" to describe our error because it is a misplacing of the correct order that causes the error. This may be an incorrect order of thinking, action, or thoughts. Let's face it: there are many ways in which we can miss it. But this is why the Word said that is [to return] to live a life that exhibits godly character, moral courage, personal integrity, and mature behavior—a life that expresses gratitude to God for your salvation, according to Ephesians 4:1. We cannot return from a place we've never gone. When we do go astray in our actions, thinking, and words, God lovingly calls us back to Him in repentance.

Finally, and perhaps more touchingly is Jesus's reply to Peter in the Garden of Gethsemane. Matthew 26:52–54 records His words,

> Put your sword back in its place; for all those who *habitually* draw the sword will die by the sword. Do you think that I cannot appeal to My Father, and He will immediately provide Me with more than twelve legions of angels? How then will the Scriptures be fulfilled, that it must happen this way?
>
> Matthew 26:52–54 (AMP)

This brief history lesson demonstrates man's need to appeal to heaven because of injustices here on earth when no such appeal will be heard. It also illustrates the role we as believers have in appealing to the lost on God's behalf and in partnership with Him. Lastly, we are to understand that our ability to appeal to heaven, as Jesus indicated, is that of a commander of legions of angel armies because we are joint heirs with Christ. We may not have the direct rank, militarily speaking, but we have the rank by association. That means we can appeal to heaven knowing in advance what is at our disposal.

In these examples, we have seen personal appeals and collective (kingdom) appeals. We see that Jesus chose not to appeal when He understood His appeal was in direct opposition to the Father's plans. He only said what the Father said, which means He pushed His own will and flesh aside if it was contrary to the Word of God. We see that Job's appeal resulted in a different kind of solution. We can all rest assured that he did not expect a double portion after all of his calamity. In both of these extremes, we know that the appeal does not come from delusion or impure motives; instead, it comes in moments of great distress submitted to a loving God.

You know you must recognize that Satan was the first person to ever be evicted. In that same tradition, we must recognize that we, as children of the Most High God, can act as agents of eviction when it comes to our enemy interfering with the plans and purposes God has for us. Trust and believe; God watches over His Word. But we, too, play a role in asking for help when we need it. He is the one who strengthens us; we are the ones who freely receive.

Now that we have established the context, if you will, through which an appeal to heaven can be made, I'd like to encourage you to throw out any thinking you may have about how to communicate in the heavenlies. This is not because God wants us to be ignorant of the things of heaven, but I believe we can get bent or wrong thinking about spiritual things and have a hard time letting go of an idea we have in our heads. I want to encourage you to lead with your heart when making an appeal to heaven. After all, Jesus did.

Consider Gethsemane again. Jesus knew the plan. The

scripture says we were all foreknown by God in heaven. That means Jesus would have not only been aware of the plans and purposes for redemption from before the time Adam fell, but He also likely took on a pivotal role in designing the plan. After all, He was the worthy sacrifice provided by God in place of the collective "us." Like the story of Abraham's test on Mount Moriah written in Genesis 22, Jesus acts as the ram in the bush, fulfilling all the Mosaic Law and the word of the prophecy concerning the Messiah. He knew about the cross and its power to redeem mankind. He even knew His sacrifice was the only worthy option, and He agreed to it. He was very clear in His mind about why He came to earth and what He was supposed to do. I believe He had counted the cost before agreeing to this redemptive plan. Yet, in a moment of despair, He cried out to His Father from His heart, not His head. Isn't this the example we should follow?

As we appeal to the unchanging nature of God, remind yourself in prayer of these truths:

- God is sovereign, and His ability to rule is steadfast.

- His desires for us are that we prosper even as our souls prosper.

- He designed us for community and honors our desires for community building because He placed those desires in us.

- Our appeals represent our hearts' cries and may be good, but God's plans are always better. We must be willing to accept a delayed "better" in place of a current "good."

- Even in our natural unworthiness, we are recognized citizens of heaven who know our Father hears our voice when we pray in secret.

Why is praying in secret such a big deal? I believe one reason the apostle Matthew brings it up is because, as a former tax collector, he understood accounting and keeping track of things. He knew through his past as an outcast in society what the cruelty of people feels like. Yet, now he was experiencing the faithfulness of God. In some ways, he gave up more than some of the other disciples when it came to material things; after all, he was a wealthy man in the world. But from glory to glory, God used his talent and peculiarity to record this sound advice from Jesus found in Chapter 6. The Word says,

> Do not let your left hand know what your right hand is doing. Your almsgiving must be done in secret. And your Father who sees everything that is done in secret will reward you.

> "Whenever you pray, do not be like the hypocrites, who love to stand and pray in the synagogues and on street corners so that others may observe them doing so. Amen, I say to you, they have already received their reward. But when you pray, go into your room, close the door, and pray to your Father in secret. And your Father who sees everything that is done in secret will reward you.

> "When you pray do not go on babbling endlessly as the pagans do, for they believe that they are more likely to be heard because of their many words. Do not imitate them. Your Father knows what you need before you ask him.

> Matthew 6:3–8 (NCB)

Ladies and gentlemen, the only word we need to speak in a moment of desperation is "Jesus." Matthew recorded our Lord's Prayer immediately following the advice to make our prayers and petitions known to God alone, and God taught us how to pray:

> Our Father in heaven,

> hallowed be your name.

Your kingdom come.

Your will be done

on earth as it is in heaven.

Give us this day our daily bread.

And forgive us our debts

as we forgive our debtors.

And do not lead us into temptation,

but deliver us from the evil one.

Matthew 6:9–13 (NIV)

Aside from Mathew, the only other Gospel to record our Lord's Prayer is Luke, the physician. It is the two professionally employed disciples, Matthew and Luke, who understood through the practice of their profession how important these words were for kingdom believers like you and I. Luke was not Jewish, which should be significant to most readers. In addition to this fact, note that Matthew was referred to as Levi when he became a disciple. His Christian name, Levi, means "Yahweh's gift." The Lord's Prayer is representative of God's gift to us even today. And out of our darkest seasons, we can partner with the consummate Gardener to plant a seed of faith in the soil of our hearts. Remember that Levi was the tribe through which the priesthood came. In other words, Jesus, in this model prayer, spotlighted not only Jews but Gentiles. He took the intentional time to acknowledge both the priest and layperson. He redeemed the outcast and used His talent to record these important truths for us.

We are *not* to be known for our many sayings or public displays of spirituality. We are commissioned, however, into ministry when we accept Christ as Savior and are duty-bound to lead as kings and priests.

There's a story from childhood the Holy Spirit reminded me

of, which I think illustrates what I am trying to say. I was a third-grade student at a small Catholic school, and I was about eight years old. We were preparing to participate in a mock Olympics, and I was excited about running in as many races as I could. My mother often reminded me that as an even younger child, I would run alongside her and my father as they rode bicycles. She also teased me because when the weather or circumstances would not allow us to be outside, I ran in circles in the small living room. I loved to run as a younger person.

I was prepared to run the fifty-yard dash at that Catholic school when the Lord taught me a powerful lesson about who we can be in Him. As students, we were expected to use starting blocks and respond in speed when the starter gun went off. Everything was very official!

As I and another runner crouched in position to begin the race, I slipped into a false start, which meant the race should be restarted. The tension I felt in anticipation of the sound of the "starting gun" going off was so intense that I couldn't hold the energy in my body still. But as I walked back to the starting line to begin the race again, the gun went off, and the other racer took off down the field. I stood there momentarily looking at the "officials" as I expected them to call her back. But they didn't. Instead, they remained silent as some in the crowd began cheering for the other racer. These school challenges were being televised on public broadcasting, and my grandmother was watching from home. I couldn't imagine explaining to her why I just stood there without competing, but I also couldn't understand why the rules were not being adhered to. As a shy eight-year-old, I didn't know what to do or where to turn to. I looked back at one of the officials again, knowing that the other racer was halfway down the track by now. He screamed, "Run!" and I did. I ran with everything I had in me, and I caught up to the other racer in a few moments. We were neck and neck for a while. My pigtails (a common hairstyle at the time) were spinning in the wind. Then I realized that despite the false start, head start, and my hair flapping in the wind, I knew I had not engaged my running reserves. I put in enough effort to catch up to my competitor and then put my effort into cruise control, not giving it all that I had inside of me. I still wasn't sure if we were even supposed to be running after the way the race began. In a brief moment, I thought of my grandmother again and decided to kick on the afterburners and win the race. So, I did. After crossing the finish line, I truly expected us to have to race again. In my mind, this little jaunt was just a warmup because there was no way it could've been considered "official."

But it was counted as "official" by those in charge of the game. Instead of winning the race, like I knew I had, the contest was judged a tie. Both of us received a first-place ribbon. In response to the puzzled look on my face, I was told, "We're ruling this a tie because you got a head start." This was as if to imply that my win was a result of cheating. It's funny now for me to think back at that injustice waged by adults against a child. And for what? Simple prejudice. I say that story to remind each of us that our enemy, whom the Jews know as Hasatan, is prejudiced against us as children of God. He will rig, misjudge, and, in any way possible, manipulate circumstances in order to steal what rightfully belongs to us. Then, like the sideline judges in that elementary competition, the evil one will try to justify or rationalize his thievery. For a short time, the scripture says, we will have to contend with his, the enemy's, verdict and spoken word over us. But like so many preaching the Word in the world today, I believe that time has come to an end.

When I got home from school that day, my grandmother told me that she watched me participate in the mini Olympics at school. She is the one who described my pigtails that twirled in spirals as I ran. Then, without comment from me, she said, "You ran so fast...you won that race!" I was shocked that she confirmed my heart's thoughts without me saying anything. "That man cheated," she concluded, "but you won." I was so excited to be vindicated, even without uttering a word. But she saw my countenance change when she began talking about the race. She knew

I had been taken advantage of by people who were making up the rules as they went along. She knew I was entitled to the reward due me as the winner of the race. To that end, let me boldly proclaim that Jesus has won the race on our behalf. He did so with flying colors, as a matter of fact. Although the enemy might question, "Did God really...?" Yes, He did! And like my grandmother in that moment, the Holy Spirit acts as a witness to the things of God so that the injustices heaped on us can be overturned. That, in my belief, is the essence of an appeal to heaven. When, like my eight-year-old self, a wrong pronouncement or judgment is running amok and causing destruction, sadness, or even delay in your life, I believe we can go to the Father and appeal to Him for justice in the situation—not with our vain repetitions, but with a contrite heart in secret.

It has been taught by more than a few that we can command the blessing to manifest in our lives, and I agree. But if we take the scripture at face value, which all new disciples would be wise to do, we see in Mark 11:23 that any one of us, you and I, can speak to a mountain and command it because Jesus gave us back the keys to this kingdom. We can also speak boldly as God commands (Exodus 7:2) in a by-proxy kind of way. We can speak commands to the things of this world, including our finances. We can speak in the commanding authority of God that has been situationally placed in our hands. The need to change a person's heart from self-destructive behaviors, needing healing from a bad diagnosis, and other such things are meant to be appealed directly to heaven.

Now, remember I commanded cancer (a mountain) to leave my body. But there are times when we are spiritually too weak to do so. We simply may not have a spiritual brother or sister to intercede for us. We may have been shaken to our core by an unexpected situation. In either case, there should be no judgment among brothers as to who can cast out what and to what effect. We have all been given the same authority through Christ, and it is in Him, ultimately in the covenant of His body and blood, that our appeals are argued and decided in heaven. No matter what the situation, we must trust in God and God alone.

SEVEN
HISTORICAL PROCEEDINGS
AND FUTURE DECISIONS

When we examine historical and modern miracles, we see the interaction between heaven and earth, which gives us a precedent for future decisions from the courtroom of heaven. As we consider these interactions, let us examine the law of first mention as a principle that guides our study. It says that to understand a particular word or doctrine, we must find the first place in Scripture where that word or doctrine is revealed and study that passage. The reasoning is that the Bible's first mention of a concept is the simplest and clearest presentation; doctrines are then more fully developed on that foundation. So, to fully understand an important and complex theological concept, Bible students are advised to start with its "first mention." The rationale behind using the law of first mention to our understanding is that it is wise to let the Bible confirm the Bible. In other words, when repentance is mentioned in Scripture, it is always referenced as being of a contrite heart. Yet examining the first stories involving repentance gives us a greater understanding of God's intentions.

Keep in mind, in this world, we only see the part and not the whole. Meaning we cannot understand all of the things of God while bound in this mortal world of sin. But we can let the Holy Spirit illuminate our understanding through study. Let's use the example of repentance, which is not only important for all believers but also vitally important for those who seek an audience in the courtroom of heaven. "Why?" you may ask. Let it be understood that when we appear before God's throne seeking a legal decision, our hands must be, firstly, free from unforgiveness and, secondly, in the spirit of repentance and submission to God. Repentance can be defined as deep remorse for past sin.

In a worldly context, it is a regret for any past action. But in the biblical narrative where the context of repentance was first mentioned, it involved turning from idolatry.

The story begins in Exodus 33. The Israelites resumed their journey in the wilderness under the direction of Moses after leaving Egypt. After miraculous signs and wonders, they were freed from a four-hundred-year enslavement and, in the process, plundered the wealth of Egypt. Imagine this walk through the wilderness in a different way with me for a moment, and really put yourself in the story.

You are walking through dry land in search of a new home. Your excitement from not having to make bricks anymore is still fresh in your mind. But you become distracted with all of your newfound wealth. Covered in jewels and rich robes, you are suddenly keeping up with the Joneses without any effort of your own. The revenge provided by your freedom represents the wealth of the nations—remember, Joseph gathered the spoils of the world during the famine on behalf of Egypt. Now, the Israelites carried that wealth into the wilderness to start a new community in a land promised by God Himself. Before you know it, you take on one of two mindsets: stubborn or rebellious.

The Israelites began to complain in stubbornness about the inconvenience of being in the desert. Others took their wealth and made a graven image to worship, yielding to idolatry. God Himself warned Moses that He would stay out of the midst of the people, only communicating with him directly because of their stubborn and rebellious nature. The Jewish nation was called a stiff-necked people (Exodus 33:3). Yet God's promise to drive out the Canaanites, Amorites, Hittites, Perizzites, Hivites, and Jebusites was steadfast. This is after the golden calf and even after He defeats the most powerful nation at the time, the Egyptians. God proved to be faithful when His people were not. This is the first time the context of repentance is given corporately in response to idolatry.

The word "repent," however, precedes this corporate context of the Exodus. It is first mentioned in Genesis 6 and refers to the grief God Himself felt when mankind turned away in sin. Verse 5 says, "The Lord saw how great man's wickedness on the earth had become, and that every inclination of the thoughts of his heart was only evil all the time" (Genesis 6:5, HCSB). It repented the Lord, or grieved Him, to see the fallen state of man's heart in the days of Noah. The first mention of the word "repent" is in regard to God's grief or repentance that He made us. When we look at the words in Hebrew, we see the word *nāham*, which is translated as "to console oneself," relent, or change one's mind. Another way of saying it is to understand God's mind as a parent. He had to console Himself for the mistakes of His creation. As a parent myself, I can relate. There are times when our children act so out of character that we have fleeting thoughts of what life would be like without them. Then, as we regain composure, we console ourselves and move forward with the plans we have for them. This is what God did with the Israelites.

God consoled Himself to stay with the original plan of having a family through the human race by saving Noah and his family. He did not forget the first seed He planted in His likeness. God honored His commitment to Adam through his great-grandson. Noah was born through the line of Seth about 126 years after Adam died. The earth was relatively new, and yet a great consequence was about to occur. But God did not forget mankind even in His judgment of us. That is important for us today as we consider the ways in which we need a judgment in our favor.

I would like to reiterate the many known signs and wonders since Jesus rose from the grave that verify His existence as not only man but God. But I'm inclined to believe that if you are reading this far into this book, you are fully convinced that Jesus was God in the flesh. I am also convinced that you would have heard of the Shroud of Turin, the recent move of God on the campus of a Kentucky college as well as the historical move of God at Azuza Street. You may also be aware of the report of oil coming from a

Bible found in Northeast Georgia for two consecutive years and the many apparitions and sightings people have reported around the world—all these events are supernatural confirmations of God's present and timely miracles in the modern world. In fact, the testimonies I've experienced in my own life are too numerous to fit in this chapter, let alone those documented around the world. These signs, wonders, and miracles are all evidence to support those future decisions or judgments in the courtroom of heaven that can be in our favor.

In an effort to link the historical faithfulness of God to future judgments in our favor, let me briefly outline the various historical eras of our faith. In order, the timeline of the church is broken into three eras: the early church, the Middle Ages, and the modern church, of which we are a part. Within those three eras are ten distinct periods that housed major movements of our faith.

The early church begins from AD 0 to 35 and continues for a little over 500 years. The apostolic century begins with St. Ignatius and the persecution of Christians by the Jews in Rome. In that period, we see the end of Nero's rulership, Christians being fed to lions, and the first great Catholic theologian, Irenaeus. Following the apostolic period was the apologist period, which lasted until AD 220. In this season of the early church, an allegorical method of interpreting scripture was introduced in Alexandria. It was also in this era that the first documented uni-church was introduced by Mani (founder of Manichaeism), who attempted to blend Persian, Christian, and Buddhist elements in what was considered, even then, a major heresy.

The early church continued through the imperial period, which concluded around AD 476 when early monks began shedding their worldly possessions and retreating to find solace in their faith. Toward the end of the imperial period, Christianity was brought to Germania, forming the Aryian Christian Church. Constantine died, and religious scholars debated the divinity of Jesus as a whole, arguing that His mind was not mortal and thereby calling into question the perfection of who we know as the perfect sacrifice.

Following this early church period came the Middle Ages, which are infamous for persecution throughout Europe in the name of Christ through the Crusades. In 431, the Council of Ephesus ruled that Jesus Christ is one person, not of two natures, as previously argued, one mortal and one divine. Rome fell, Pope Benedict added the Holy Trinity to the Nicene Creed, Muslims retook Jerusalem, and the church remained divided for roughly 1,000 years.

In 1500, the Reformation kicked off the modern church age, with Martin Luther nailing his 95 Theses to the door of the Wittenberg church after seeing the corruption in the church. He was subsequently excommunicated about ten years before John Calvin's conversion to Christianity. In other words, the modern church is as tumultuous as the Middle Ages but far more enlightened. In fact, after the Reformation, the Puritan period began, which was followed by the Great Awakening. The King James Bible was printed in 1611, Presbyterianism was founded, and various acts of "uniformity" were drafted, including the Book of Common Prayer, in an effort to unite the church. Revivalists took center stage in 1800, in Kentucky, thirty-six years after the Baptist denomination was founded. Methodists reached beyond their parachurch founding. By 1816, the first African Methodist Episcopal (AME) church was founded by Richard Allen. Throughout the 1900s, several significant events occurred that contributed to the contemporary Christian movement, including the death of Dietrich Bonhoeffer and the publication of Christian metaphysical thrillers by J. R. R. Tolkien and C. S. Lewis. Evangelist Billy Graham's conversion and subsequent crusade ministry played a major role, as did the rise of the television evangelist movements that led to major networks being owned and operated by Christians. In the education arena, former seminaries, Harvard and Princeton, were lost to liberals and unitarians, and the Scopes Monkey Trial ensued. Politically, America witnessed the election of the first Catholic President, John F. Kennedy, and his eventual assassination. Other deaths marked the century, including the assassination of Rev. Dr.

Martin Luther King, Jr. Prayer was officially removed from American schools in 1962, and abortion was legalized a decade later, along with the loosening of morality laws against same-sex unions. These events all either censure or celebrate the church.

Although most church timelines continue to categorize the 2000s as part of modern church history, there is a concerted effort of sorts to recognize the post-modern era we may find ourselves in today. Take note that post-modern does not mean post-Christianity. Pastor John Hagee, Senior Pastor of Cornerstone Church in San Antonio, Texas, and the founder of the Zionist organization Christians United for Israel (CUFI), often presents a powerful timeline of Israel, God's time clock. Understanding the history of Israel is key to understanding the historical proceedings that lead to future decisions for us, spiritual Israel, who are grafted in sons and daughters of God Most High.

Many of us may be aware of the promises God gave to Abraham, the father of faith, as outlined in Genesis. When Abraham left his homeland to go to an unknown place because of a prompting from God, he became the first person to leave the polytheistic traditions of the pagans in order to establish what would become the Judeo-Christian faith. Abraham's father, Terah, was an idol maker in the town of Ur of the Chaldeans. The lifespan of most people dramatically decreased as the earth became more populated. God scattered men by language after the Tower of Babel, and mankind increased on the earth. I have often imagined what it was like for Abraham to respond to God's draw. A glimpse of the conversation is found in Genesis 12:1–3.

> The Lord had said to Abram, "Go from your country, your people and your father's household to the land I will show you.
>
> "I will make you into a great nation,
>
> and I will bless you;

I will make your name great,

and you will be a blessing.

I will bless those who bless you,

and whoever curses you I will curse;

and all peoples on earth

will be blessed through you."

Genesis 12:1–3 (NIV)

Unlike Abraham, we have countless hours of formal teaching about God available to us on any number of media, our personal devices, in print, and in the theater. Abraham had nothing but a gut check in response to hearing God in his heart. Certainly, God had primed the pump of his hearing by revealing the futility of his father's work. I can imagine Abraham, even as a young man, questioning his father and the practice of idol worship. "These graven images do not speak. Why should I bow to them?" he might have said. At his father's rebuke, he might have replied, "Are you not God since you created the gods we worship?" Certainly, the dichotomy of living in a home financed by idolatry was not lost on him. After all, when he left Ur for Canaan and then settled in Haran, a city named after his deceased brother, he was already married and childless. The text does not tell us how long Abram (as he was called at that time) had been married, but it may have already been known that Sarai, his wife, was infertile. This would have been a major conflict in those days and still can be today. Infertility is something medical science has only recently brought solutions to. In Abraham's day, it was akin to a curse. Sarai not conceiving would have caused Abraham to cry out in his heart for an answer. God most likely began revealing Himself to Abraham in the everyday things around him, just like He does with us.

God is always speaking. As was stated in a previous chapter,

God will use our environment to speak to us—to point out the fallacies in our thinking. It is how we respond to this prompting, this revelation, that can be a determinant of future decisions and judgments of God's favor.

Let's reconnect with this one central theme of why we exist on this planet. We were created to love and be loved by God Almighty as part of His holy family. We are intended for the purpose of magnifying Him as Creator and ruler of all things seen and unseen. We are meant to worship Him. These facets of loving and serving God are the principal reason why we were created beings in His image. Second to this divine design is to love our neighbors as ourselves. Giving and receiving love is at the origin of our birth and should be the focus of our lives.

Abraham lacked this to a certain extent because he was childless. Being image-bearers means we innately desire the same things God desires. Abraham wanted a family, and when he realized through the influence of God's omnipotence that idolatry could not rectify that longing—that the idols his community worshiped could not solve his problem—he began to look elsewhere. Most likely, he witnessed animals and plants reproducing, and God quickened his understanding. "Am I not more valuable than them?" he may have wondered. "Yet they reproduce after their kind, and I cannot."

If there ever was an argument for the need for a godly witness, mentorship, or the need for a forerunner, this is it. Psychologists use the term "associationism" to describe the response to stimuli and complex mental processes, which include thinking, learning, and memory. As early as the time of the Greek philosopher Aristotle in 384 BC, theories involving man's ability to determine similarities and differences and act upon those associations were studied to determine the approach people take to their environment. Abraham recognized the lack of offspring as being more than just undesirable; it was abnormal in the order of nature. On a basic level, he understood that he and his wife were engaged in an activity that should produce a desired result, and since they were met with failure, something unexplained was happening. This unexplained phenomenon, infertility, was at one time accredited to sin. Before medicine and science offered insight into any condition, people quickly laid blame at the door of the afflicted person. How often do we read in the Bible, "Who sinned? Him or his father?"

From the Garden of Eden forward, we seem to want to place blame and identity wrongdoing on a person rather than on a set of circumstances that have various nuances. This is a byproduct of Satan's deception, in my opinion. We point the finger, just as Adam did, in order to (1) make sense of things and (2) divert responsibility from ourselves. But if we want God to respond to our needs, to satisfy the questions and longing we might not even have words for, we must respond as Abraham did, by faith. To all these expressed groanings, uttered and unuttered questions, to the murmurings in Abraham's heart, God spoke to Abraham's heart, and he responded in the only appropriate manner, which is obedience.

In 1 Samuel 15, the prophet admonishes King Saul that obedience is better than sacrifice. At the time, the king was in a rebellion against God, who placed him in the seat of authority. His "sacrifices" were but vain, posturing to appear pious, but Samuel actually rebuked the king. When God tugs on our heartstrings, He looks for an honest and obedient response, which He credits to us as righteousness. Face it; none of us has the strength, wisdom, or charisma to make ourselves righteous. But, like Abraham, we can be credited with righteousness through our obedience in faith. Anything less than an obedient response can result in a rebuke by God.

One last thing to remember regarding future decision-making by God is He has a divine plan that cannot be thwarted. We may understand some of God's plan just by being in tune with the things around us that are created by God. For example, we can see fruitfulness and multiplication all around us in nature, so it should not be difficult to believe in that promise. We may also understand more specifically if we have a relationship with the Holy Spirit, the person who reveals the heart of God. We can also hear the words of a word sent by God, like Samuel, the prophet who was sent to correct King Saul, who can direct us in the way we should go, sharpening us like iron. Of course, we have the Bible to act as a representative of God's authority and plan for humanity, which must confirm all other revelations.

Ultimately, no matter how we hear from God, our only caveat must be to know that His plan is the final authority on everything. Deviating from God's plan is not only ineffective but also rebellion and disobedience. In a manner of speaking, it is idolatry—the literal situation Abraham left when he chose to follow God. We must make that same choice. Knowing in our hearts that God's Word is the final authority. Knowing that it is rooted in love. Knowing that it is inextricably tied to the character of God Himself and, therefore, God's Word cannot be undone, ineffectual, or erroneous. God's Word is not only true but also alive. Obedience to God's Word is the most practical means of future decisions in our favor because God rewards those who diligently seek Him.

Consider again Abraham's situation. Not only did God answer his plea for a child, but He did so abundantly, making him the father of many nations. God financed Abraham's mission to become the father of faith by providing for him as Jehovah Jireh. When his nephew, Lot, fell into a dangerous situation in the city of Sodom, God sent angels to intervene because Abraham asked Him to. In other words, through obedience, Abraham developed a friendship with the Creator of the universe, having access to petition on behalf of the lives of others. What great power and authority is given through faith. God has not changed since those days. He still expects obedience from His children. As Abraham did with regard to his faith in God's Word, we must do, also.

Those of you who know the story of Abraham understand that there were times in which Abraham failed to be faithful, either to his wife, the promise God gave him, or to his own character. God's plan prevailed through Abraham's human failure, which can bring relief to us today. God does not expect perfection; He expects obedience.

There was one particular time in my life when I grew weary in waiting for the promise to be manifested. Remember, Abraham had to wait and, in his weariness, ended up with Ishmael as an illegitimate son. When I first heard my personal promise from God, I begged Him not to make me wait as long as Abraham did. (Frankly, I didn't think I could be faithful for twenty years to wait on a promise.) But I dare to say that God does not delay us for no reason. His timing is perfect. Sometimes, that perfect time comes when we finally learn to be obedient. Other times, perfection may be determined by the other circumstances that must occur to execute God's plan most efficiently. Moreover, there may be other reasons why we experience delays. But like in Abraham's story and countless others, including my own, God's promises do not fail. Wait for the appointed time, write the vision, and make it plain so that you can hold onto God's Word because it will come to pass if we faint not (Habakkuk 3). In other words, God always provides the confirmation or reaffirmation of the promise when we diligently seek. We will be found (or heard) by Him, and He will sustain us when we grow weary in the waiting. Future decisions by God are always based on His past performance. Where He has been faithful in the past, He will be faithful in the future because He is the same yesterday, today, and forever. All His promises are yes and amen.

> For God shows no partiality [no arbitrary favoritism; with Him one person is not more important than another]. For all who have sinned without the Law will also perish without [regard to] the Law, and all who have sinned under the Law will be judged *and* condemned by

the Law. For it is not those who merely hear the Law [as it is read aloud] who are just *or* righteous before God, but it is those who [actually] obey the Law who will be justified [pronounced free of the guilt of sin and declared acceptable to Him].

Romans 2:11–13 (AMP)

We who believe God are chosen to fulfill God's Word on the earth. This is assuredly secured by our faith in Jesus Christ.

EIGHT

THE COURT OF
THE TABERNACLE

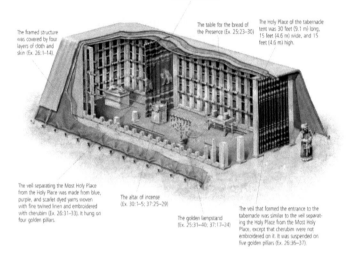

The Most Holy Place was a 15-foot (4.6-m) cube, containing only the ark of the covenant (Ex. 25:10–22; 37:1–9). It was here that Yahweh would descend to meet with his people in a cloud theophany (divine appearance). The high priest could enter only once a year, on the Day of Atonement (see note on Heb. 9:7).

The table for the bread of the Presence (Ex. 25:23–30)

The Holy Place of the tabernacle tent was 30 feet (9.1 m) long, 15 feet (4.6 m) wide, and 15 feet (4.6 m) high.

The framed structure was covered by four layers of cloth and skin (Ex. 26:1–14).

The veil separating the Most Holy Place from the Holy Place was made from blue, purple, and scarlet dyed yarns woven with fine twined linen and embroidered with cherubim (Ex. 26:31–33). It hung on four golden pillars.

The altar of incense (Ex. 30:1–5; 37:25–29)

The golden lampstand (Ex. 25:31–40; 37:17–24)

The veil that formed the entrance to the tabernacle was similar to the veil separating the Holy Place from the Most Holy Place, except that cherubim were not embroidered on it. It was suspended on five golden pillars (Ex. 26:36–37).

Image by www.langleychristianassembly.com

As much as I have considered myself a student of the Tabernacle, I read something new about it, which, in hindsight, I see as obvious symbolism created by God. Blogger Justin Taylor compared the Tabernacle to the Garden of Eden based on three distinct areas of the most holy place on earth outside of the person of Jesus Christ. He proposed that the Tabernacle, which is symbolically presided over by two bronze cherubim on the ark of the covenant, mirrors the two angels who were placed at the gate of Eden when Adam and Eve were evicted. Taylor suggests that the Tabernacle was the place of God's dwelling when the Israelites were in the desert, which is backed up by scripture, just as Eden was the place of God's dwelling before the fall of man (Exodus 25:1–31:17). The documented parallels of east-facing entrances, trees, gold, and knowledge, Taylor points out, are evidence of God's continuing covenant with mankind and the infallibility of His Word. One way to note this parallel is to understand fully that what God says, He means. While the court of the Tabernacle does not serve the same functions as the other courts I have discussed so far, it is still an important place for us to comprehend it as a representation of both the Holy of Holies in heaven and on earth. The Tabernacle, called *Mishkan* in Hebrew, was a portable sanctuary in the wilderness constructed per the instructions of God as a tent with an inner and outer court. These areas are described in elaborate detail in the Old Testament. The Word records that the outer courtyard was flanked by a rectangular fence containing the altar of burnt sacrifices. It makes sense that God's BBQ grill is in the outer courtyard, but what we might not have recognized is that the smoke from the burnt offerings would have been observed from a great distance off. Two million Jews lived in the wilderness.

The sight of the smoke from the altar would have been seen as an indicator that worship was taking place in the camp. This can be powerful if you dwell on its understanding. Many congregational churches of the early nineteenth century used a steeple bell to announce the call to worship. Other religions use a type of horn to signal the time to worship. Modern churches use music or a countdown clock to let congregants know when the service is about to begin. But in the wilderness, it was smoke from the brunt of sacrificing that yielded a powerful silent cry to come before the altar. From miles away, the smoke would have been visible to anyone with eyes to see. Like an incense, the smoke stretched up toward heaven.

Make a courtyard, Exodus 27 says, with an altar built of acacia wood, and let it be flanked on each corner with a horn overlayed with bronze. Curtains of finely twisted linen in purple, blue, and scarlet shall be hung around the courtyard on posts that stand twenty cubits high, which is almost three stories high. The Tabernacle, like God Himself, is bigger than we think. This was an imposing edifice the Jewish nation put up and took down several times as they traveled in the wilderness. Deuteronomy 17 references the Tabernacle's courts for the cases Levitical priests would have heard from the people on their journey to the land promised by God. As we look into this segment of Scripture, get a picture in your head of your own promised land. Use your imagination to recall what God has spoken to your spirit and turn your eyes upon Jesus. Perhaps it is a divine calling and purpose. Or you may be believing for physical healing. Another common desire is for us to have a loved one return home from a prodigal adventure. Others seek clarity, love and companionship, abundance in finances, peace, emotional healing, and restored identity. In other words, if you were approaching the Tabernacle for a court decision today, what Bible-based promise would you bring before the Lord? Whatever it is, get a picture of it in your mind as we travel into the Tabernacle.

In this passage addressing the king and those in leadership over Israel, the Word makes a reference to inferior courts when speaking of those issues and complaints not brought before the Sanhedrin. The Sanhedrin, if you recall, was the group of elders who were called to pass judgment on Jesus prior to Him being turned over to the Roman officials for crucifixion. These powerful men acted as rulers over people and presided over court proceedings in an inferior courthouse, called the Lesser Sanhedrin, and an upper house called the Great Sanhedrin. Deuteronomy 17, biblical scholars say, was written to reference the Great Sanhedrin as those judges who ruled at the Tabernacle. The original Sanhedrin, those who judged in the wilderness Tabernacle, were charged with making legal decisions that involved blood against blood and plea against plea (verse 8). These cases were referred to the high priests and decided in a "place" the Lord God chose. These are cases the blood of goats and bulls cannot cover and claims only Jesus's blood can attest to. This imagery cannot be more clear. Whether before the judge or the High Priest of the Lord thy God, we must recognize that the blood of Jesus speaks a more perfect Word. In the high court of the Tabernacle, we can plead the blood.

I want to join you in agreement for the thing that you might be believing God for. Know that if you have received a word in your heart or believed a word written in God's Word, then you are a candidate to have the blood of Jesus work on your behalf. There is no greater healing balm. No greater victory than that that is found in Jesus's sacrifice. As co-heirs with Christ and as co-laborers in these final days before Christ's return, let us join hands on earth as in heaven to partner with the blood for a victorious decision in the court of the Tabernacle.

Precious Lord,

You have fully given of Yourself

Therefore, we fully give _____ [your area of need or concern] to You,

Knowing that You have our best interest at heart and are working diligently to bring about the victory in our lives.

We plead Your blood over our circumstances.

We plead Your blood over our family.

We plead Your blood over our nation.

and we plead Your blood over our own will

so that we might be obedient to Your call,

Effective hearers of Your Word,

Walking in forgiveness and godly love.

Thank You for Your blood and the opportunity to Tabernacle with You as Your will is done on earth as it is in heaven.

Amen

NINE

THE COURT OF THE PRISON, PARDONS, PAROLES, AND DECREES FOR BREAKTHROUGH

When I was in my early twenties, pregnant and unmarried, my younger brother, who had been my best friend, went to jail. Except for a ten-year stretch, he was in and out of jail or prison for the remainder of his natural life. I say "natural life" because my brother came to faith before he transitioned into the heavenly realm, and I believe with all sincerity that he is dancing on streets of gold right now. That being said, because of my brother's story, I have spent a lot of time associating with the prison system. I've been the witness for the defense and the constant visitor. I've written the appeal letters and met with lawyers. I've been the one to pick someone up after a long sentence, and I've also been there when the cuffs have been put on. I've been as close as anyone wants to be to being behind bars. But besides all that, I have also been detained myself.

On a cold December day, when my daughter was still in diapers, I was pulled over by an officer while on the way to work. My mother and an infant sibling were in the car with me. She'd planned on borrowing my car while she babysat my daughter. Per my morning routine, I passed a police precinct on my commute. On this particular day, a woman in a convertible sped past me, switching lanes without signaling. I remember thinking, *Someone needs to pull her over before she hurts someone.* As the thought was still attached to my mind, blue lights flashed behind me. I continued to drive for a block or two, assuming the officer was going after her and simply needed me to move over so he could protect and serve. Eventually, I realized I was being pulled over. Just what I needed—a delay that might cause me to be late for work. As I pulled over, the officer followed me. Minutes later, there were three vehicles lined up on the side of a busy thoroughfare.

Unfortunately, that day I unknowingly left my wallet at home. Although the officers were able to verify the validity of my license, they could not verify proof of insurance because a high-speed chase nearby jammed the frequencies, which would have allowed me to go free. As the laws were enforced at the time, no identification and no insurance meant jail time. I begged the officers to call my office, a building I could see from the side of the road where we were detained, to verify my identity so I could get to work. Again, no calls would connect. In what I considered to be a quick decision, the officers called a tow truck, took me to jail, and put my mother out on the side of the road with two toddlers, neither of whom was wearing a coat. Let me remind you, it was December.

All reasonable people used to say, "If you are Black in the South, make sure you are respectful to police officers just in case you run across one with an itchy trigger finger." Well, the same might be true no matter what color you are. That day, being driven away in handcuffs while my infant child was exposed to the December cold when she and my mother were left on the side of the road, I had no intention of respecting anyone. In fact, I pretty much did what any mother would do—I went ballistic. I railed and screamed and cried. Then, I began to pray aloud and sing songs of praise. Don't think I was super spiritual at that moment. I was such a baby Christian that there was little evidence, in the natural, that I was even saved at all. I began to pray because I assumed that only a demon would leave a child on the side of the road like that, so I was determined to cast that demon out of that officer by the Word of God.

Now, unlike some who have run-ins with the law, I didn't lose my job because charges were dropped when my credentials could be verified. Unlike some, I was able to get my car back from the impound in a timely manner. Unlike some, I recovered. But I know of many people who end up in jail or even temporarily detained like I was that day and have cyclical repercussions from their encounters with law enforcement.

You might say that if you don't do anything wrong, you won't end up in jail. Well, I just told you about my encounter with a traffic officer who decided I was a danger to society and arrested me because I couldn't prove who I was. This officer could have let my mother drive since she had her license with her. This officer could have waited until the high-speed chase was over so he could verify the validity of my insurance policy. He could have also admitted that he pulled me over without cause. Disregarding all of the options common sense might have recommended, the law in Georgia stated that a person without identification and insurance found driving a car could be arrested. There was a legal precedent that allowed me to be detained. Had I known that someone might consider me a menace to society because I left my purse at home, I would have taken the time to make sure I was carrying identification. Matthew 24:43 (NKJV) reads, "If the master of the house had known when the thief was coming, he would have stayed awake and kept watch, not letting his house be broken into." In other words, we can be detained, delayed, and even jailed because of ignorance, legal precedent, and common decisions that leave us open to the wiles of the enemy. It is that last category I believe can be answered by God in decrees for breakthrough.

WHAT IS A DECREE?

From the Latin word "to judge" or divide, a decree is a judicial decision of a court of equity or a judgment in a court of law. According to Noah Webster's 1812 dictionary, decrees in theology are a predetermined purpose of God, whose plan of operation is, like Himself, unchangeable. As powerful as these definitions are, consider that the word "decree" is also a transitive verb that is referenced in Job 22:28 (KJV), saying, "Thou shalt decree a thing, and it shall be established." It is to determine or resolve legislatively, to fix or appoint, to set or constitute by edict or in purpose. In short, to decree is to determine judiciously to resolve a sentence. When I was arrested for having a bubble in my tire (this is what the officer documented as my reason for being detained), I was charged with driving a malfunctioning vehicle. Hours later, the charges were dropped, and I was released; I believe God honored my decree even though I had no knowledge of the power of confession to change my circumstances. I simply wanted to irritate that officer or the demon I thought was using him to the degree that he would let me go just to get some peace. But as I understand it now, words have power. Even though I didn't know what I was decreeing, it still went to work for me in my life.

To this scripture, Job commentator Alan Clarke writes, "When the heart prays, God hears." Oftentimes, we pray only in our hearts, and the mercy of God, in His omnipotence, answers. Without petitioning the Father, whether in our hearts or aloud, we need not be surprised if we do not receive an answer from the Lord. The scripture reminds us in John 14:13 (NKJV), "Whatever you ask in my [Jesus's] name, that will I do, so that the Father may be glorified." This word is confirmed by Matthew 7:7 (NKJV), "Ask and it will be given you, seek, and you will find, knock, and the door will be open to you." We must cast our cares on Jesus for He cares for us (1 Peter 5:7), having confidence that those concerns which we bring before Him, if asked in His will, He hears (1 John 5:14–15). Finally, believers, I urge you to be anxious for nothing. Instead, bring everything to God in prayer and supplication with thanksgiving. Let your requests be made known to God. And the peace of God, which passes all understanding, will guard your hearts and minds in Christ Jesus (Philippians 4:6–7).

Based not only on our natural understanding of the legal system but with the scriptures referenced above, it seems pretty clear to me that power comes when we orally cry out to God in prayer. As in Psalm 107 verse 28, when they cried to the Lord in their trouble, He brought them out of their distresses. One thing I know for certain, people in prison lack peace. When the legal system has passed judgment on a person, binding them, the only one who can help in those moments of desperation is Jesus.

Time and time again, we are bound in a prison in our minds, finances, physical bodies, and emotions. Who can answer these pleas except Christ?

No one, of course. But when Jesus left this earthly realm, He gave us the authority to speak as He did. That is why I believe an oral decree is a powerful authority we have been given in this realm to break the captives free, even ourselves.

For the past year, I have been a partaker in an online ministry through an app called Clubhouse. Decrees for Breakthrough, led by Apostle John Eckhardt and a group of powerful intercessors from around the United States, leads listeners in a series of decrees based on God's Word every weekday morning. The practice of decreeing aloud God's Word over our lives and needs has broken prison walls, led to pardons and paroles, and set us up for breakthroughs in every area concerning us. How can I say this with confidence?

One thing is true for me personally. I received a download from heaven fourteen years ago concerning the calling heaven has for my life, a calling that, at the time, I had no ability to walk in because I was still an untrained, bound believer. I used to mumble to myself in times of distress, things like "I'm afraid... This or that." I might recant the problem and try to work out my own solution. Many a time, my thought life and meditations of my mind were on the problem, not on God as my solution. I was in a state of victimhood. Practicing decrees for breakthroughs has changed my verbal mutterings and my thought life, which was dramatically transformed when I accepted Jesus as Savior. Let me be clear to point out that for me, it has taken years to undo the stinking thinking I had about myself and my purpose. But as I was trained, I fell into alignment with God's Word. As I agreed with the breakthrough, I began to see it manifest. Even when I didn't see the breakthrough, God still deserved the glory. My hallelujah belongs to God even on the journey to breakthrough because He deserves all the honor for the work He is actively doing in us.

From the first time I heard the Word of God concerning me

until now, the only spiritual discipline I acquired was agreeing with the promises in the Word aloud, with decrees for breakthrough. I'm sure that mutterings in my heart were heard by God because the Scripture confirms that God hears. But my acting in greater boldness and participation by decreeing a thing out loud has accelerated my freedom in various areas of life, like parole.

As previously mentioned in this book, there are legal loopholes Satan uses to bind us. We, too, have a legal option called the decree for breakthrough. It is almost difficult to imagine breakthrough being just one decree away and the millions of men and women who could be freed from their bondages in a moment in time.

While I do not believe there is a separate courtroom for prison, paroles, and pardons, I use the term to illustrate the fact that as we seek freedom, a judicial decision is made in support or in opposition to that decree. That is why it is vitally important for us to agree with God's Word often and aloud, by faith. There is a myriad of examples in God's Word about being bound in prison. The most talked about of these is the story of Joseph, found in Genesis 39. Something I never focused on when I first studied this book was the fact that Joseph was put in a special section of the prison that was used by the king's prisoners. How many of you know that when a king is pivotal to a biblical narrative, we need to discern the correlation between both earthly kings and spiritual kings in a prophetic manner?

Archeologists have confirmed evidence of a great mass of people who were known to be Canaanites moving into Northeastern Egypt and the Eastern Nile Valley and "taking over from within." These people were eventually expelled from Egypt and settled in a land later known as Judea. Modern Egyptology refers to these people as Hyskos, who are portrayed as invaders and oppressors in the Aegyptiaca, a journal of Egypt's history. We do not need to be Egyptologists to understand that the word Hyskos comes from the same root as the word hyssop, which is referenced in the biblical narrative of the Passover found in Exodus 22.

"Take a bunch of hyssop, dip it into the blood in the basin and put some of the blood on the top and on both sides of the doorframe. None of you shall go out of the door of your house until morning" (Exodus 12:22, NIV).

I want to make plain what I feel the Holy Spirit has revealed about the word Hyskos because there are many people who try to disprove the Bible as a historical text, the motivation for which can only be to disprove the existence of God (which is an exercise in futility from my point of view). Many Black Americans have had conversations in their hearts and with others concerning the historical representation of slavery and the achievements of African Americans in the building of the United States. Black scholars, researchers, businesspersons, and others who have reached a level of comfort in this nation are uncomfortable with the fact that misrepresentations, either through covertly diminishing the impact of Black America or overt erasing our history in a process called "whitewashing," exist in the history books used to educate our future leaders. In fact, there have been a number of contributions to the great American experiment that were given through the hands of Blacks that are not taught in schools, stories no one knows about. There is a devious reason why these stories have been left out of public view. Let me not delay the point any further. People who are ignorant of history are bound to make mistakes, operate in further ignorance, and have little historical impact. That, my friends, is the motivation behind keeping Blacks and others ignorant of the historical accomplishments of all of America's Founding Fathers. How else could you justify the three-fifths doctrine? How else could our nation make Jim Crow palatable in textbooks? How else can marginalization continue? Power, greed, and the isms of our world have presented versions of history for their own narrative. Yet, it is not just in America where this has occurred.

Hitler, a fan of the Ku Klux Klan, also rewrote history between World War I and II in order to brainwash a generation of Germans into believing the Jews were the cause of their problems. Thus, the

German solution to rid the world of Jews was able to flourish into the Holocaust. Under the control of Ugandan dictator Edi Amin, the Acholi and Lango ethnic "cleansing" took place to the cost of 500,000 lost lives. And long before the International Criminal Court began hearing crimes against people, despots and potentates from around the globe have murdered innocent people from AD 132 to the writing of this book; people are being killed for their ethnicities. In the 21st century, the Nagorno Karabakh's Armenian population, Ukrainians in the Russian-occupied territories, Tigrayans of Ethiopia, Rohingya Muslims, Kurds, Christians, Yazidis, and other minorities in Turkish-occupied northern Syria, the Uyghurs in China, the Bodos in India, the Tamils in Sri Lanka, Uzbeks in Kyrgyzstan, and African Americans in Azuza, California, have been the victims of some level of ethnic targeting resulting in the deaths or displacement of more than three million people. At some point in the local histories of each of these nations, the people in power will tell their version of the story that documents this time in history, and it may not convey the unadulterated truth because sometimes the truth is ugly. It is unkind. It causes repentance. Truth can set you free, but it can also cut you. So, how can we assume that the Egyptian story of the Hyksos is not the ancient Hebrews who left Egypt under the leadership of Moses, along the floor of the sea after painting their doors red with the branches of hyssop? We cannot, and we should not.

Back to Genesis 39. Joseph is thrown into prison after a false accusation. While there, he meets a butler and a baker of the king. Joseph's ability to interpret dreams by partnering with the Holy Spirit furthers his reputation, which eventually reaches the king's ear. In a matter of days, he is taken from the prison to the palace. This is a story many church-trained believers know inside and out. But have we ever considered that as the eleventh son of Israel (Jacob's anointed name), he represents the eleventh-hour deliverance of the people? Joseph also represents grace, mercy, and providence. God did not come when Joseph may have wanted;

after all, he spent years in prison for a crime he did not commit. On the other hand, God did show up on time.

When we consider our circumstances, whether we are imprisoned by negative thoughts, financially in the prison of debt, or bound in our physical body, we must understand that we have an eleventh-hour deliverer. Like the Israelites under Joseph's leadership and those who left Egypt under Moses, God is taking us safely to the other side.

So, let's reason together with God concerning how we can use decrees to our advantage. As previously stated, we can be detained, delayed, and even jailed because of ignorance, legal precedent, and common decisions that leave us open to the wiles of the enemy. When we differentiate between being detained and being delayed, we get a deeper understanding of the power of a decree. To be detained is to be restricted, restrained, or bound. Many believers find themselves bound by tradition, being preoccupied with rules or laws from the old covenant, and treating faith as a list of dos and don'ts. While I believe in repentance just as much as I believe the sun will rise today, I know many are caught up in legalism instead of falling in love with God through relationship. By proof of God's Holy Spirit and the Word of God, we can understand that Jesus came so that we could be one with God. I believe God wants us so fused to Him that we are not distracted by the mistakes made against us or by us. Instead, we are satisfied with pressing on to the high calling, knowing that, at times, we will stumble. But as we grow in God, our stumbles become less frequent and ultimately less devastating. I believe that is what is meant by 2 Corinthians 3:18: going from glory to glory by the Spirit of God. Feel free to disagree with me, but I know the mistakes I make today, after growing in my relationship with the Lord, are far less devastating than the mistakes I made when I first came to Christ. He has taken my life from glory to glory, and I can't praise Him enough. Would you say the same is true for you?

Sometimes, believers are bound in addiction or other wrong thinking, which can cause a delay in purpose. I find that this often comes from a false identity. You may believe God is real and that He is love, but for some reason cannot reconcile His love to yourself. Perhaps this is because you have not truly accepted your identity in Christ. In fact, I'm willing to wager that at least half of the people on Earth have not accepted their identity in Christ, maybe more. Why? Because if we did, we would not be out there doing what we do to people and ourselves. The judgmental, unloving way we interact with others is not a reflection of Christ—it reflects our flesh. This judgment can lead to addiction. This judgment can lead to self-loathing and hatred toward others. In other words, it can lead to the destruction of purpose. That is not what God wants for us. So, if you or someone you know is bound up in this cycle of wrong identity, do not stop interceding for them. Pray scripture over them, calling them by name. For example, Deuteronomy 28 lists some of the promises of God that, with diligence, will yield fruit when we listen to the voice of God. It brings chain-breaking anointings. Please know when we say chain-breaking, we are talking about prison chains.

PROMISES OF GOD

You *will be* blessed in the city, and you *will be* blessed in the field. "The offspring of your body and the produce of your ground and the offspring of your animals, the offspring of your herd and the young of your flock *will be* blessed. "Your basket and your kneading bowl *will be* blessed. "You *will be* blessed when you come in and you *will be* blessed when you go out. "The Lord will cause the enemies who rise up against you to be defeated before you; they will come out against you one way but flee before you seven ways. The Lord will command the blessing upon you in your storehouses and in all that you undertake, and He will bless you in the land which the

Lord your God gives you. The Lord will establish you as a people holy [and set apart] to Himself, just as He has sworn to you, if you keep the commandments of the Lord your God and walk [that is, live your life each and every day] in His ways. So, all the peoples of the earth will see that you are called by the name of the LORD, and they will be afraid of you. The Lord will give you great prosperity, in the offspring of your body and in the offspring of your livestock and the produce of your ground, in the land which the Lord swore to your fathers to give you. The Lord will open for you His good treasure house, the heavens, to give rain to your land in its season and to bless all the work of your hand; and you will lend to many nations, but you will not borrow. The LORD will make you the head (leader) and not the tail (follower); and you will be above only, and you will not be beneath, if you listen *and* pay attention to the commandments of the Lord your God, which I am commanding you today, to observe them carefully. Do not turn aside from any of the words which I am commanding you today, to the right or to the left, to follow and serve other gods.

Deuteronomy 28:3–14 (AMP)

When I was interceding to free myself and my family members from the chains that bound them, I focused on this passage from Deuteronomy 28. Each time I read or recited the scripture, I inserted the names of those I prayed for into the text itself, knowing that this spiritual labor was not in vain. I had faith, believing that this discipline would have an impact, not just be Holy Ghost lip service. Take verse 14, for example, "Do not turn aside from any of the words which I am commanding you today, to the right or to the left, to follow and serve other gods." I would say aloud, "*I* [insert the name of your loved one here] will not turn aside from any of the words that God is commanding me today. *I* will not turn to the right or to the left [away from God] to follow or serve other gods." Then, I might add that I will love the Lord with all my heart, mind, and soul (Mark 12:30–31). Figuratively put your foot in the Scripture and bind it to yourself so that the enemy will have no authority to bind you or your loved one. God has not promised us everything, but He has promised that anything we ask in Jesus's name, according to His will, He hears.

Imagine a child calling their parent's name repetitively. How long does that child go unacknowledged? Not long, I suppose. Perhaps that is why we are commanded to seek God, to seek an audience with Him so that we may be heard. His desire is to commune with us in fellowship and conversation. That is the foundation for decreeing a thing (anything) so that it may be done. Why else would Jesus have given us a model prayer based on a decree? *On earth as it is in heaven.* That phraseology alone suggests decrees. When we call things that are not as though they are, aren't we decreeing a thing? When we petition with thanksgiving, thanking God as if He has already answered our cry, is it not with the expectation that a decree in our favor will be granted? Many of us have been decreeing for years, not realizing the power of the words we have spoken. These prayers of petition have legal authority in the earthly and heavenly realm for sons and daughters of the Most High. They can lead to paroles and pardons. These decrees can lead to breakthrough. In fact, that is the only way God wants us, ultimately free.

As we petition God in prayer, we must remember that He has given us numerous examples of the ways in which we can plead our case before Him for supernatural intervention. We can request stays of judgment, ask for pardons and paroles, and even plead with God to overturn judgments against us and our bloodline. In doing so, we must know without a shadow of a doubt that the audience we have with the Father is made possible only through the Son. "There is no other way," Scripture says in John 14:6, "to the Father except through Me. I am the way," Jesus said, "to truth and life." Pleading the blood of Jesus in the spiritual courtrooms of heaven is a very biblical practice. Partnering with the Spirit of God to overturn circumstances and change mindsets is the relevance of our calling in these last days. And as we enter into the last of the last, let us remember that it is with prayer and thanksgiving that we make our petitions known to God, with praise. As we have done all we know to do about a situation in our hearts, the Bible instructs us to stand therefore.

"Therefore" is also a legal term related to decisions and judgments of a court. Just like the "whereas" and the "resolved" in a petition or proclamation, "therefore" precedes the decision of those in authority. In Matthew 9:29 (ESV), Jesus said, "According to your faith let it be done unto you." Romans 12:3 (NIV) seems to confirm these thoughts by adding, "Think of yourself with sober judgment, in accordance with the faith God has distributed to each of you." To each man is given, the Word of God says, a measure of faith. I'll remind you that man means mankind, both male and female, in this text. So, by that same gift of faith, believe in Him who is "the author and finisher of our faith" (Hebrews 12:2, KJV). Poetry aside, God desires that His children be made whole. He offers us a path to wholeness through His Son, Jesus. In Him and by His blood, we are given an audience with the Father. The Holy Spirit there, in that audience, acts as advocate and counselor.

God is the only one we deserve to ask for help because, let's face it, in most circumstances, He is the only one who can help. He reminds us that we belong to a kingdom system, which is mirrored here on earth. That kingdom system has keys to open heaven on earth and keys to God's vision. The keys unlock our hearts and minds to know God more and, in turn, understand how His kingdom system works.

Let's look at a practical example most of us can relate to. In the travel industry, there are a certain number of pricing blocks set aside by the company. When John Q. Traveler attempts to make a reservation, he will see pricing blocks available to him based on his level of membership or the organization's need to move inventory from one level to another. For instance, travelers with a brief history might only see rack rates for travel. These are the standard, no frills included, rates the company values their product for. Other travelers who belong to a frequent flyer or other affiliation might see rack plus additional discounted rates for which they are eligible. As our value to the organization increases, our booking options increase and more pricing blocks become visible to us. The fact is, those other levels were available all along, but most of us do not see them because they are hidden from us. When I was booking rooms for my timeshare, I kept trying various date and location combinations trying to find what I was looking for. Eventually, I realized that the inventory I saw and the inventory available were based on my level of ownership. I could only see what I was eligible for. In God's kingdom, the same is true. We are eligible for all, ultimately, but we can only see what we are spiritually disciplined to see. God does not limit us; however, the enemy will illegally attempt to at every turn. Even in this regard, we can petition heaven and agree for our breakthrough in Christ by decree.

Let us partner together in faith for the breakthrough you seek.

Heavenly Father, we come to You as children, decreeing what You have said about us in Your Word. We acknowledge Your love for us and the power to change the atmosphere through Your Spirit. We acknowledge our baptism by faith in Jesus Christ. Grant us, Lord, the petitions of our hearts and the meditations of our minds that we might fulfill Your purposes on earth. And concerning those things which we cannot bear alone, we call on You. You said in Your Word that You would make us the head and not the tail, above and not beneath. You said You would command the blessing upon us and that we would not lack. Therefore, we agree and trust in Your promises to see us through any adversity. We decree the breakthrough according to Your Word, asking that it be done unto us as You have said. In Jesus's name, amen.

When we pray in Jesus's name, believing in the "amen," it is as if the proclamation has been stamped not with red wax and a seal from a clerk but in the blood of Jesus and sealed by the Holy Spirit for all eternity. That, as Jesus said on the cross, it is finished.

THE END

BIBLIOGRAPHY

Locke, John, *Two Treatises of Government*, Edited by Mark Goldie, Everyman, 1999

ABOUT THE AUTHOR

Lisa Noel Babbage is an educator and philanthropist who works with several nonprofit and civic organizations, including The Christian Association of Public Theologians (CAPT), No Left Turn in Education, Rotary International, Voices Against Trafficking, and Culture of Life 1972. Through Maranatha House, her own nonprofit organization, Babbage has provided temporary and emergency housing for single females. In partnership with the Atlanta Union Mission, Babbage participated in a multi-year feeding outreach to our communities' most needy. Recently she has led a series of talks bent toward strengthening the Black community.

An author of more than twenty-five books and a documentary filmmaker, Babbage was born in Philadelphia and raised in an Old Fourth Ward housing project in Atlanta. She is the mother of two and a proud grandmother. She is also a member of her local church, serving for more than a decade as a camera operator and member of the production team at Free Chapel Worship Center, as well as a teacher in their Restoration Ministry. Babbage is a Lincoln Civic Spirit Yeshiva Fellow, a former DeKalb County Teacher of the Year, a NAACP Sutton Education Scholar, and part of the inaugural beneficiary class of the National Science Foundation Waterman Award partnership with Georgia State University and Gwinnett County Public Schools. She resides in Gwinnett County, Georgia.